THE CRAFT

THE CRAFT

A Guide to Making Poetry Happen
in the 21st Century

Edited by Rishi Dastidar

Nine
Arches
Press

The Craft
Edited by Rishi Dastidar

ISBN: 978-1-911027-85-0
eISBN: 978-1-911027-86-7

Cover artwork: © Ria Dastidar, Uberpup
http://www.uberpup.net

First published November 2019 by:

Nine Arches Press
Unit 14, Sir Frank Whittle Business Centre,
Great Central Way, Rugby.
CV21 3XH
United Kingdom

www.ninearchespress.com

Printed in the United Kingdom by:
Imprint Digital

Nine Arches Press is supported using public funding by Arts Council England.

Supported using public funding by
**ARTS COUNCIL
ENGLAND**

CONTENTS

Part Two: On Making Poems

Part Three: On Bringing Poems to Life

FOREWORD

Rishi Dastidar

For so many of us, 'craft' is a word that is double-edged when it comes to writing poetry.

It is a necessary word of course – what art can be done well without a grip on the basics of the technique of its creation? And who, at whatever their level of proficiency and facility, does not want their work to be 'well crafted', to be of the highest possible quality that it can be, achieving the goals that they have set for themselves?

But 'craft' is a slippery beastie too. Many of us – especially those of us from backgrounds where poetry writing is not a common way of spending time – are more than familiar with the whisper, the critique, the rejection that, while the work is *good*, it is in some way lacking in some aspect (often not articulated) of craft. And it can become a way of excluding people from the art, through suggesting ideas of standards that are unclear to beginners – and even to those who have been writing for a while.

This collection of essays is an attempt, not to supplant craft in poetry or overthrow it, but rather to broaden and deepen what it means in the 21st century – making it live for all poets, no matter what tradition you're writing in and from. This is, necessarily, a political act, but one with a small p, and – to my eyes at least – there is nothing contentious in the book.

And for the avoidance of doubt: in no way does this volume replace guides to writing and learning about poetry such as those by Stephen Fry and James Fenton[1]. The Fenton is a foundational text for me, and it's a volume I come back to when I need to be reminded of how pentameters dance and

---

1   Stephen Fry, *The Ode Less Travelled: Unlocking The Poet Within* (Arrow, 2007); James Fenton, *An Introduction to English Poetry* (Penguin, 2002)

dactyls land. I want you to read those books too, and gain that knowledge and understanding.

But then I want you to recognise that, to write poetry today, you need to be thinking about more than just your technical, prosodic abilities. How do you perform your work? What about the ethics of using real life in what you write? Can you use technology as a way to push your work to new places? These are 'craft' questions, as much as knowing how to get the most out of a sonnet, attempting your own translations and improving the titles you give your poems – all subjects covered here.

I also feel obliged to point out that this is not a traditional 'how to' book: while there are practical tips galore in these essays, I have deliberately avoided drawing them out where the writer has chosen not to themselves. But within the personal stories and opinions you will find insights as to how to approach poetic craft in such a way so that your writing is renewed with a new spirit; and perhaps you will develop a sense of loving the process of 'crafting' – after all, the best part of writing is working and reworking and working and reworking and working and reworking your words.

My thanks to all the contributors, for their time, generosity and creativity in sharing aspects of how they work, and to Jane Commane in inviting me to edit the guide.

Let me close with an analogy with a world I know well, that of branding and corporate design, where I spend my non-poetic days. The logos that my colleagues in the design team make all start with a pencil being picked up, then sketching – squares are drawn, curves swoop, circles connect. But very quickly they take these sketches and start to recreate, remake and remix them in computer programs like Photoshop and Illustrator, using the power of those to vividly bring their ideas to life. In how they approach their task, they start by using what you might call traditional craft skills – but then they have to use newer approaches and thinking to get to something that works for today.

The point being, of course, that ideas of what craft is, what it might be and what it can do never stand still. And that's as true for poetry as it is for any other creative endeavour.

And you must learn the rules – new and old – in order to break them. Happy writing.

Nine Elms, London
October 2019

INTRODUCTION

Do All Rabbit Hutches Look Alike? Against 'Craft' in Poetry

Will Harris

"Of all things of thought, poetry is closest to thought, and a poem is less a thing than any other work of art." – Hannah Arendt, *The Human Condition*

1.

A poem isn't a rabbit hutch just because they look the same from a distance. By which I don't mean that poems and rabbit hutches look alike, but that to the untrained eye all poems look the same and all rabbit hutches look the same. Their samenesses, though, are different.

We're taught that poems have certain formal features in common: rhyme schemes, iambic pentameter, "summer's lease hath all too short a date". But really they can take any number of forms and do what they want – have one-word lines or no lines, include dialogue and pictures, even be in prose.

A rabbit hutch is limited by form in the real sense that if its form changes too much it's no longer a rabbit hutch; if it fails formally it fails completely. The food tray might be badly placed or the gate's faulty lock might cause it to swing open at the slightest nibble. If so, the craftsman has failed.

Rabbit hutches are defined by their form. Poems only make use of – or avoid – forms and techniques. A poem could decide to set itself political, moral or aesthetic goals that it fails to communicate or realise, but in an important, literal, sense poems can't fail.

As Wallace Stevens put it, "poetry is a revelation in words by means of words." (Imagine how a tradesman would react if you told them a wardrobe was a revelation in wood by means of wood.)

Though I say this now, for a long time I was under the thrall of craft. Maybe I was scared that someone was going to expose my lack of it. At university I spent two months on a poem that began: "A necklace of stem that's easy to snap./ A thinly hairy stem of granny's nightcap." I pored over its sound patterning and rhythm, repeating "thinly hairy" over and over again in my head. I was stuck.

I thought that, as with building a wardrobe or fitting a horseshoe (things I definitely can't do), the more I practised the better I would get. But 'real' craftsmen work with materials that have consistent properties. If you heat up or hammer metal it reacts in a consistent way. No one pulled me aside to explain that writing a poem isn't like that; poems don't just improve over time corresponding to effort.

More than that, no one pulled me aside to explain that 'craft' was a misapplied metaphor. It takes formal or technical features, embedded in a particular cultural-linguistic tradition, and then extrapolates them into a false, pseudo-mystical idea of what poetry *should be*. It's about granting access and denying entry.

What do we mean when we say some poems are "beautifully crafted" and others "lack craft"? Who decides what value should be placed on any given set of formal features?

Instead of saying poems should have evenly-spaced vowel sounds and an internally consistent thematic domain, what if we said that all art should be done in felt-tip pen and applied directly onto the flank of a cow? Because that's how it felt to me back then. Trying to write my long poem featuring a "thinly hairy stem of granny's nightcap," I thought that the more the cow squirmed and the pen slipped, the harder I needed to push. Resistance showed I was on the right track. So I didn't stop to question why I was knelt beside a cow holding a felt-tip pen in the first place. This was *craft*.

2.

The Poet's Freedom by Susan Stewart begins with an anecdote about a trip to the beach where she describes seeing a small boy building an elaborate sandcastle replete with turrets, crenels and a little moat. Having finished, the boy steps back to admire his work and then runs at the castle and proceeds to kick and stamp it to pieces, smiling all the while. Stewart writes:

> Since then, that boy has represented for me a certain relation we have to making. Without the freedom of reversibility enacted in unmaking, or at least always present as the potential for unmaking, we cannot give value to our making. Was his castle a work of craft rather than art – one he felt could be replaced easily? Did this object that implied, but could not realise, an interior acquire an interiority in being a memory alone?
>
> By destroying the mere thing, and using all his physical might to do so, the boy seemed to be returning the power of the form back into himself, as if what he had been practicing all along was a mode of memorisation or, better, learning. Once the skills used in making the castle in its entirety were internalised, they were ready to be used again. Unwilling or unable to be the curator of his creation, the boy swiftly returned it to its elements, that is, to its pure potential.

I take from this a kind of parable about the differences between craft and art, or about the dialectic that exists between the two. With craft, you're making something that can be replaced – a commodity. If you spend all day building a wardrobe and then someone comes along and smashes it, you'll be angry because that wardrobe represented a day's work and could have been used or sold (it was also unique in its way) but the power to remake it is still inside of you. In fact, as that boy on the beach discovers, you might find your power affirmed in the act of its destruction.

With art objects, broadly defined, there's a quality of irreplaceableness. If you rewrote the *Divine Comedy* it would be a different poem. The art object is defined by the threat of destruction in a way the craft object isn't. Its terminal fragility is the site of its value. And whereas the destruction of the craft object proves the strength of the maker, the (possible) destruction of the art object proves the strength of the work. It affirms what Stewart calls its "interiority", the vital flame of its inner life.

But the division between art and craft isn't clean-cut because, of course, the maker is crucial to the work of art, and the alternating impulses towards art and craft are generative. Seeing them in dialectical terms should bring out the risks of an excessive focus on either. Too much art leads to a vatic emptying out; an abnegation of ethical responsibility. Too much craft leads to a narrowing of vision; the production of mere commodities.

When I was obsessed with craft, I thought there were models I could imitate that would show me how to make and remake indestructible little poems like stainless steel spoons. But putting together a poetry book I've realised just how insufficient good writing is. What's important is that the work has that sense of "pure potential". A life that exceeds itself. Which lives because it can be destroyed. Which wants to live through others.

Because a living thing is much more than a crafted thing. It can't be bought or sold or replaced. It's death-aware, shaped by the same "freedom of reversibility" that shadows our lives. It tells us that we're more than just form; it tells us to cradle, for as long as we can, the potential that defines us.

3.

Reading Kamau Brathwaite's *History of the Voice*, I rediscovered a poem I'd forgotten about by Derek Walcott called 'Blues'. Often I find it hard to know whether I like a poet's work. It can take me by surprise when something clicks. It was a while before Walcott clicked for me, and then it was less because of anything I'd read by him than because aged 18 – around the same time I was writing "granny's nightcap" – I heard an old recording of him reading 'Blues', a poem about a nighttime assault in New York City. This is its first stanza:

> Those five or six young guys
> hunched on the stoop
> that oven-hot summer night
> whistled me over. Nice
> and friendly. So, I stop.
> MacDougal or Christopher
> Street in chains of light.

It looks like a conventional poem: lines of equal length, a clear (though loose) metrical tick, a compound adjective ("oven-hot"), and rhymes (guys/nice, stoop/stop, night/light). But said out loud it's transformed. Or not transformed, which suggests changed. Rather its submerged rhythms float up to the surface. In Brathwaite's essay he says you can hear in Walcott's voice "the sound of Don Drummond's trombone". Drummond was a key player in the ska scene in Jamaica in the 1950s and 60s and perhaps Brathwaite is saying that, although 'Blues' is a poem about an assault, it sounds as joyful and raw as a trombone solo.

Listen to that languorous first sentence ("Those five or six young guys"), the way it unfolds over four lines before coming to a halt: "So, I stop." The trap has been laid; we know where this is going. But the poem's narrative[2] doesn't tell the whole story. Rather than describe the fight, the speaker talks about his

---

2   Read the poem in full here: https://engpoetry.com/derek-walcott/blues/

new sports-coat, which he hangs on a fire-plug for safekeeping: "They fought/ each other, really." His voice conveys a mixture of presence and absence; pride and shame; he's physically welded to the moment but detached from it emotionally.

He saves his sports coat and crawls up a flight of stairs. You can hear the bite as he mimics the mother of one of his attackers and tosses aside an explanation for the violence ("nothing" coming in again; the same qualifying "really"). Understanding doesn't always entail sympathy. But the reason the speaker can be so detached – so absent – is because he doesn't care about these "young Americans"; they're already ghosts to him. He's listening to the tune playing in his head, the sound of his own voice.

Brathwaite gives 'Blues' as an example of "nation language". In contrast to dialect, which is defined by its deviation from 'correct' English and so subject to caricature, nation language expresses a "submerged, surrealist experience and sensibility." Brathwaite talks about growing up in Jamaica surrounded by the language of the planter, the official, and the Anglican preacher, the works of Jane Austen and Shakespeare – the "contours of English heritage" everywhere, stifling expression. He mentions the child who, never having seen snow, writes: "the snow was falling on the canefields." No one writes about hurricanes. "We haven't got the syllables, the syllabic intelligence, to describe the hurricane, which is our own experience," Brathwaite writes, "whereas we can describe the imported alien experience of the snowfall." Nation language, for him, means aligning syllabic intelligence with actual experience.

A poem is "a revelation in words by means of words." I think it's that sense of language revealed to itself I responded to in Walcott's reading of 'Blues', the feeling of someone finding a language to fit their experience. Though the poem may use elements of craft, it doesn't rely on them – it exceeds them. Received forms carry the dead weight of sentiment, and this is poetry that wants to blow away sentiment, to answer those questions raised by nation language: *What is the hurricane in your life? How will you make your language adequate to the contours of your experience?*

4.

Amiri Baraka once said in an interview that "no amount of attention to craft will make anybody write beautiful (or whatever) poems." But I don't think the point of craft is beauty; it's mastery. The craft analogy treats the English language as if it were a consistent material like wood; it suggests that with the correct training and models (a 'canon' of great works) language will submit to the maker's will. But what lies at the end of mastery? "Nor shall Death brag thou wander'st in his shade,/ When in eternal lines to time thou growest."

Against the lure of "eternal lines", Baraka tells poets to trust "what notes come under the fingers as an improvising musician." When you improvise, the tune may die as soon as it's played but at least it's yours. Its beauty lives in context.

For my work to live I had to abandon a strict adherence to craft. I had to question why I'd put such store by the correct models, in being correct, and what lay behind the fear of failure. I had to discover context, to trust in it. And context is more than just writing about what you know. It's more than a corrupt polity or the last cheese single in your fridge or what you can see from your kitchen window (a rabbit hutch, say) or how your grandmother died. A poem might include all of those things – maybe should – but first it has to embrace the inevitability of its own destruction. Be written not to posterity but to the present moment. Because a living thing is much more than a crafted thing.

PART ONE

ON POETIC FORMS

I Will Put Chaos Into Fourteen Lines and Keep Him There: On the Sonnet

Jacqueline Saphra

I have so often wished with all my heart that there was another fixed form that could do what the sonnet can do: by which I mean, pretty much anything. The first passable sonnet I ever wrote was early in my poetry life: I'd been experimenting with free verse and was beginning to grasp the idea of the central importance of the line in poetry. But like a child in a superstore, I was overwhelmed by the lack of boundaries and too much choice.

When I came across *The Making of a Poem* by Mark Strand and Eavan Boland, I was captivated by the chapter on sonnets and I pored for hours over the example poems. They all had a discernible magic in common that seemed connected with the form despite having been written centuries apart. Yet each was unique although all were bound by a commonality of structure and certain challenging rules. How could that be? From Milton to Elizabeth Barrett Browning, Edna St Vincent Millay to Mary Jo Salter, each sonnet hit me viscerally and emotionally before I began to consider the complexities of argument or progressions of thought. It was as if I'd started listening to a playlist of songs I had always known and loved without realising it. The iamb (an unstressed syllable followed by a stressed one: *dee-dum*) sounded its heartbeat drum. The pentameter, of five iambs together, felt like a single exhalation blowing along the poetic line[3]. I was waking up to the possibility of an infinity of self-expression in one satisfying, neat little square of text with its inbuilt music. I wanted to understand how it was done, I wanted to do it

---

3   For some helpful technical instructions for writing sonnets, visit
      https://poets.org/text/sonnet-poetic-form

myself, I wanted to be Prospero, I wanted the book of spells. I read sonnets obsessively from Shakespeare to e e cummings to Marilyn Hacker and I drove myself to distraction trying to make them work for me.

So my first proper sonnet emerged from a single image; it was that rare and welcome recipe of emotions that elicited a poem based on one sustained metaphor. I was standing in the kitchen with my oldest son who had just turned thirteen when I realised he was taller than I was.

Outgrown

Back to back we stand in ritual
of measurement. My first born, ticking clock,
my gangling hourglass, my wake-up call,
we stay, four-footed, steady as a rock.

Hold fast and then release. Now there's the trick.
I see it still – your embryonic hand
waving through water in a magic lake –
you, fishlike, still a million years from land.

My long-limbed journeyman, my wayward friend,
as surely as the life-lines on my face
one more sweet story draws towards its end –
this new one leads you to a separate place.
Outgrown, I'll watch you scale the dizzy heights
on giant feet, your face turned to the light.

This is a classic and obedient Shakespearean structure – a variation on the love poem – with its *ababcdcdefefgg* rhyme scheme; you can hear some Bardish tones echoing in some of those phrases. Looking at it now, it's certainly grandiose in its diction, somewhat adjective-heavy and cliché-laden, but it already dares to let go of full rhyme and it feels solid enough in its construction. When I'd finished it, I felt as if there had been some discovery and surprise as part of the process, but I knew it wasn't nearly good enough and I wanted to do it better.

Reader, I was hooked.

The sonnet is unique and exquisite in its capability to marry feeling and thought. This is not to say it's easy to work with. Those rhyme schemes and the infamous iambic pentameter can trip you up. You can't afford to let any syllable be unnecessary or forced; you have to watch excessive use of the adjective or conjunction as filler. You have to think about what kind of sonnet it is, its shape and trajectory. The Shakespearean sonnet, with its ladder-like rhyme scheme born of the rhyme-poor nature of the English language, demands the slow unfolding of an argument in four quatrains with its neat little couplet at the end, so unfashionable in this age of irony and lack of answers. And yet how satisfying when the poet offers us a conclusion, a summing up, a perfect insight:

> So long as men can breathe, or eyes can see,
> So long lives this and this gives life to thee.
> – Shakespeare, Sonnet 18

> And he will be the one to stammer, "Yes."
> Oh mother, mother, where is happiness?
> – Gwendolyn Brooks, 'Sonnet Ballad'

Edna St Vincent Millay, an early poetic role-model of mine, born in 1895, and one of our greatest and most innovative sonneteers, would often use the final couplet with a clever feminine rhyme with comic and devastating effect:

> Some sane day, not too bright and not too stormy,
> I shall be gone, and you may whistle for me.

Millay excelled at the earlier, Petrarchan sonnet structure, drawing on its counterbalanced octave (eight lines) and sestet (six lines) which require a kind of proposition and answer, with that oft-vaunted volta – or turn – just beyond the middle point. Millay wrote hundreds of sonnets in her lifetime, charting her stormy love affairs and disappointments and the process of ageing, taking what had been essentially a form created for and dominated by the male viewpoint and writing from a female perspective. She constructed sonnets in her head, reportedly, sitting curled up in an armchair, before she ever started to write them down. Millay knew how to use the slow progression of the closing sestet in the Petrarchan sonnet to create a work so moving it's almost unbearable to read. One of my particular favourites of hers is simultaneously a love poem and a meditation on the ecstatic challenge of the sonnet itself. I relish the volta exactly at line nine, where there is a temporal shift from future to present. In the octave, Millay announces her intention – and in the sestet, her intention is realised: "I have him". The man was more tricky than she let on, but the form: she has the form.

> I will put Chaos into fourteen lines
> And keep him there; and let him thence escape
> If he be lucky; let him twist, and ape
> Flood, fire, and demon — his adroit designs
> Will strain to nothing in the strict confines
> Of this sweet Order, where, in pious rape,
> I hold his essence and amorphous shape,
> Till he with Order mingles and combines.
> Past are the hours, the years, of our duress,
> His arrogance, our awful servitude:
> I have him. He is nothing more nor less
> Than something simple not yet understood;
> I shall not even force him to confess;
> Or answer. I will only make him good.

Embedded in your bones

When people say they feel as if form prevents them from expressing themselves, I counter with: what might happen if you set yourself the task of writing, say, an extremely tight, formal Shakespearean sonnet with full rhymes? What might you learn from working with regular pentameter, a rhyme scheme, that slow development of the argument over four quatrains and then the challenge of that final, ringing epigrammatic couplet? Have you felt the joy of creative constraint, the way an iamb might push you towards a certain word with the required stresses, rather than the word that first comes to mind? Have you experienced the jolt of discovery, when you have to find a rhyme – Rilke called rhyme 'a goddess of secret and ancient coincidences' - and suddenly the poem takes you in a direction you haven't expected? Don't you long for that feeling that is so rare and enlivening when your poem begins to write itself? Form can do that for you. You just have to practise.

Most of us have tucked away in our files many more failures of poems than successes; these are often just the rehearsals for poems to come. Think of yourself as an athlete practising a high jump over and over again, taking the falls and risking the blunders, until you know how to find your footing, how to balance your weight in the upward leap. Any skill is partly a matter of experience and partly a matter of trust. Let the sonnet work its magic on you and embed itself in your bones.

Once the sonnet is in your bloodstream, that may be the time to attempt the sixteen-line Meredithian sonnet, as in his coruscating sequence *Modern Love* or perhaps a curtal sonnet[4], the thrilling invention of Gerard Manley Hopkins. If you're feeling super-adventurous, give yourself permission to dispense with rhyme, or abandon the pentameter altogether. Not because you can't write in iambic pentameter, but because you choose not to for good, poetic reasons of form and content needing to work in synergy. What about an acrostic sonnet of thirteen lines, as Frank O'Hara's full throttle 'You are gorgeous and I am coming', written to Vincent Warren, love of his life, or one like Edwin Morgan's 'Opening the Cage: 14 Variations on 14 Words' where the same words in a different order appear in each line? Or even go for a poem that simply pays tribute to the spirit of the form in its proportions but doesn't necessarily conform to its rules.

---

4   See https://poets.org/poem/pied-beauty

Generally I've found the sonnet a particularly useful container for rage or extreme political polemic, as in my poem 'Spunk' from *All My Mad Mothers* in which I rewrite the creation myth from Genesis, or 'Leda and the Swan', my answer to Yeats' poem of the same title in my collection *Dad, Remember You Are Dead*[5]. You can see how I've progressed from the obedient and somewhat derivative *Outgrown*: note the way I let the stresses wander just a little a bit along the line:

Leda and the Swan

'How can those terrified, vague fingers push
The feathered glory from her loosening thighs?' – WB Yeats

It's nothing new: beast of a man beats
a woman, traps her, skirt round her waist,
thighs pinned under the fake webs of his feet.
Come fist, come blade, this man is not the first
to claim a metamorphosis. The violence is here,
not in a bardic prelude to some greater war.
How can she reclaim the timeless tale of man
as god? Not in her given role as poet's whore.

Show me the *knowledge*, William Butler Yeats.
Show me the *great wings*. There are none.
Only a rapist who thinks he's god, who takes
because he can. No so-called *heart*, no *glory* then.
Fuck that. Fuck Atreus, fuck Agamemnon,
fuck Zeus, motherfucker masquerading as a swan.

Next time you feel angry, I recommend you write a sonnet: there's immense power and safety in the sonnet's pressure-cooker design.

Your biggest, boldest imaginings

If, perchance, one fine and surprising day, you find the single sonnet is not capacious enough to hold the theme you're

---

5   You can read my further discussion on the writing of this poem on the Nine Arches Press blog: https://bit.ly/2NlHGkF

exploring, consider the sequence. Marilyn Hacker is as skilled a sonneteer as you'll ever find – have a look at her erotic sequence of love poems in *Love, Death and the Changing Seasons* or Rita Dove's collection *Mother Love*, a retelling of the story of Demeter and Persephone. For pure and true rule-shattering, read Terrance Hayes' transcendent and political collection, *American Sonnets for my Past and Future Assassin*. Or why not attempt the classic crown of sonnets: seven sonnets where each one takes as its first line the last line of the previous one? Or if you're grappling with a giant theme, try the heroic crown: gorgeous, expansive and inspiring, this is a sequence of fifteen sonnets where each one begins with the last line of the previous one, and the fifteenth sonnet is made up of the first lines the previous fourteen. For a great example, read Marilyn Nelson's devastating *A Wreath for Emmett Till* or George Szirtes' autobiographical, atmospheric *Portrait of My Father in an English Landscape*. The heroic crown is an exquisite challenge: mind-blowing, obsessive, infuriating, delicious; I did it in my biographical ekphrastic sequence after the photographer Lee Miller, *A Bargain with the Light*. When people say it's a hard thing – all those rhymes! – I remind them that you never have to face the blank page, because each sonnet starts with the last line of the previous one. This is a form that can give shape to your biggest, boldest imaginings.

The sonnet offers a strategy to structure your insights, thoughts and feelings, not to mention the outpourings of your unconscious, into a form, which, paradoxically and because of its very dependability, never does what you expect. Infinitely malleable, infinitely musical, that fourteen-line distilled shot of pure poetry is a gift: free, beautiful and limitless in possibility.

Enter the Fun Matrix: On Writing Sestinas

Marvin Thompson

1. What is the point of writing sestinas – aren't they tricky and annoying?

Sestinas provide me with a framework for writing better poems. This is because their strict pattern of repeating end words forces me to make poetic choices that I would not normally make. However, there is a caveat. Writing a sestina can be like breakdancing whilst wearing a straightjacket. Sounds near impossible, right? What if we were to loosen that straightjacket, just a little?

Traditional sestinas originated in 12th century Provence and were used by troubadours – performers who travelled around medieval France, singing and reciting poems.

In the following sestina schema, the numbers represent the stanza and the letters represent the end words.

1. ABCDEF
2. FAEBDC
3. CFDABE
4. ECBFAD
5. DEACFB
6. BDFECA
7. (envoi) ECA or ACE

The three-line envoi must also contain the remaining end words, BDF.

What's my experience of the form, and why am I keen to teach you the intricacies of sestina composition? I have published ten different sestinas, and have been writing them regularly over the last five years. This is of course bettered by the esteemed Patience Agbabi, who has published countless more, including her sequence of seven sestinas, 'Seven Sisters'. I mention this because Agbabi's book, *Transformatrix* (Canongate, 2000) is a masterclass in the art of sestina construction. Buy it. Read it. Read it again.

And to those of you asking, "Why is a Black, 21st century poet meddling with such an archaic, European verse form?", firstly, since I write in a European language, it is probably just as well that I appropriate European verse forms for my own mischievous ends. Secondly, if sestinas weren't worth using they would have become extinct centuries ago. Thirdly, European forms are human forms and, guess what I am…

2. Initial planning

Before writing a sestina, there is planning to do. Of course, you could just jump straight in, but is that any way to build a house?

As a writer of narrative poems, I always look to character in my initial planning phase: who is the main protagonist? For help with this, check out Will Storr's, *The Science of Story Telling*, (William Collins, 2019). From Storr I have learnt that believable characters will have a particular world view which will get them into trouble – not necessarily cops and robbers trouble, but definitely psychological trouble.

My planning will revolve around the main character's particular world view, where the narrative is set and what particular problem the main protagonist is facing. Will she overcome her problem (happy ending) or not (sad ending)? Moreover, I consider how the events of the story will leave my main character changed. For each sestina, I complete much of this work in my head through days of thinking at odd times of night. Note-taking would probably make this process more efficient.

Of course, whether you are writing a lyric, narrative or abstract sestina, there is likely to be research to undergo. Let it lead you to unexpected horizons.

3. Choosing your end words: the mix-and-match approach

Due to my success with sestinas, you may think that I have a fail-safe system for choosing my end words. Sorry, I don't. However, my favourite method is what I will call the mix-and-match approach. This means using all of the tactics detailed below in a kind of fluid, organic swirl.

It pays to remember that you should enjoy writing sestinas – part of that enjoyment comes from the challenge of finding end words that work for you and your poem, words that excite and delight.

4. Choosing your end words: the thematic approach

On the surface of it, choosing the following words: fire, heat, red, burning, danger, flame for a poem about an arsonist might seem wholly appropriate. However, especially if you are writing a narrative poem, such close focus on one theme can be reductive. As you are perhaps beginning to understand, the trick with sestinas is to find as much flexibility as possible within the knotty, seven-stanza framework.

I can hear you shouting now: "Marvin, surely the end words will become the thematic sauce of the poem because they are repeated!" This is the point – the thematic approach to choosing end words needs some care. Should a poem about an arsonist only consist of words relating to 'fire', or do you want to add humour to the character? Perhaps not. However, with some cod psychology, you might realise that the end word 'father' now turns the tale of an arsonist into a story with psychological depth.

5. Choosing your end words: the write-the-first-stanza-and-see-what-happens approach

My three-sestina sequence, 'The Baboon Chronicles', started out as a prose poem. The best prose poem ever written, a prose poem that was so brilliant that it wasn't rejected, it was ignored. So then I was convinced that the poem should be a sestina! Not really, I was only guessing. However, once I'd written the first stanza, I was persuaded that a sestina was the correct form for this particular tale. Perhaps the outlandish scenario of Britain being overrun by baboons needed a deeply sobering form to actually sell the story to readers. Perhaps.

So here's how I wrote the sestina version of 'The Baboon Chronicles.' With the first section of the prose poem on screen, I copied and twisted the material until I had the first stanza of the sestina. Along the way, the flabbiness in my prose was corseted by the sestina's structure. Once I finished writing the first stanza, I looked over the end words. Were they suitable for a sestina?

Let's take the end phrase 'White neighbour' from the first stanza of 'The Baboon Chronicles.' Was 'neighbour' a flexible end word that would withstand repeated use? I didn't think so. However: 'white'? Bingo! At this point, I said to myself, "Go on Marvin, be subversive. Use 'white' as an end word but don't end with it!" Was this a subversion too far? The full line could have read like this:

> Do you also extend this kind of hospitality to your new White
> neighbours?

In the above example, the line break comes after 'White'. The end word is positioned correctly but the line lacks elegance. Usually, you want a line of poetry to make sense on its own. Moreover, the line break does not make for an effective dramatic pause. It's a poor line of poetry.

As a result, I took a deep breath and wrote this:

Do you also extend this kind of hospitality to your new White neighbours?

The above line does the job of a grammatically correct sentence. It makes sense on its own. It conveys meaning with very little fuss. And yes, the end word, 'white' is not at the end of the line. Naughty.

6. Choosing your end words: the homophones, homographs approach

The potential for boring your readers with a sestina is huge. You have all these words being repeated – the same words that you would hunt down and delete if used more than twice in any other poem. So how do you keep these end words fresh?

Homophones can help. Let me indulge myself with a short anecdote: I once discovered that the word 'rays' has something like 15 different homophones – words that are spelt differently but sound the same. I set about writing a poem where all the end words were a homophone of 'rays'. The poem was rubbish. But oh, the fun I had writing a rhyming poem that only had one rhyme.

With sestinas, homophones become powerful tools because, even though the words sound the same, they have different meanings. You could even call them BOGOF (buy one, get one free) words. For example, choose 'mourning' as an end word and you also have 'morning' to play with, thus expanding your possibilities.

Other BOGOF words are known as homographs. Here is an example from the end of stanza one and the start of stanza two of my sestina 'This is Only an Example, Folks!':

and then I handed my wife a rose.

As noonlight seeped through the stained glass, she rose
from her pew and kissed me.

What's not to love about homographs? All this playing with
language beats three hours on the Xbox, hands down.

7. Choosing your end words: the idiomatic approach

blood red / blood moon / blood pressure / blood orange /
bloody mess / bloody hell / blood clot / bloodclaat
(*a bit rude there, sorry*).

Above is a list you might add to your planning notes once you
have decided that 'blood' is one of your end words. Idioms
are great if you are using the sestina form to write a dramatic
monologue. They give your lines the feeling of real thoughts
or speech.

How about this list?:

child / childbearing / childish / childhood / children / kids /
kid gloves

As you can see, there is lots of fun to be had with choosing end
words that you can manipulate to your own maleficent ends.

8. Editing

If you've read this far, you may be expecting more jokes and
witticisms. I'll try. Editing can be a dry subject. Water pistols at
the ready...

After weeks of work on your beloved sestina, to read your final
draft and cry, "Fiddlesticks! The end-word pattern in stanza
two is wrong. The whole poem is out of order." Of course, you
could leave the poem as it is. However, here's how to ensure
you use the correct pattern of end words. Write and edit your

first stanza. When you are happy with your results, write out the end words for the remaining stanzas in the correct order. This can be done on screen or on a separate page in your notebook. Now you have a visual guide for your end words. Magic!

Even with all your efforts, you may find that some of your lines lack a certain something. You could try pre-modifiers. For example, when editing my sestina, 'Leila', I used the following pre-modifiers to enliven the end word 'girl':

shop girl / **reticent** girl / **my** girl

Much of the delight I receive from writing sestinas is this playfulness with language that they demand.

Another sestina-focused editing tip concerns what I shall call 'show-offy' words. These are the words that stick out like a sore digit. Strangely, I am often oblivious to the destructive nature of my own show-offy words. It takes a good friend/mentor/editor to point them out to me.

When editing 'The Baboon Chronicles,' my editor at Peepal Tree Press made it clear that using the word 'baboon' 21 times over three sestinas was a no-no. "What!" I exclaimed. "These are sestinas. The word 'baboon' must be repeated!" Of course, I was wrong. Never let a form's traditions – or the strictures of a personal form that you have made up – get in the way of a good poem. In the end, we used rhyme to add variation. Consequently, the word 'baboon' became 'loon,' 'rune' and 'moon'.

Oh, and when writing an envoi (the last stanza of a sestina), I ignore the end word pattern completely. I just make sure that the envoi contains all six end words.

A sestina is a poetic matrix built for fun. It's as much about the writer enjoying the process as it is about the reader marveling over the end product. Also, sestinas are a classic example of using a form to help you construct something new rather than posing a tricky, cryptic puzzle. The laws of a sestina were made to be modified. To prove this point, I have deliberately extended my seven-section sestina essay into eight sections. In the same way, in 'The Baboon Chronicles,' each envoi has four lines instead of three. Subversive!

The Sense of Distillation:
On Prose Poetry

Carrie Etter

Early in my teaching career, I wanted a definition of poetry expansive enough to include as many types as possible, from experimental to prose to sonnets. Considering Gwendolyn Brooks' declaration that poetry is life distilled, I settled on the following: A poem combines distillation (focus, concentration, etc.) and musicality. It is through the intensity that comes with focus and musicality (that may come from metre, repetitions of sound, speech rhythms, etc.) that we recognise poetry.

How do prose poems fulfil this definition? They achieve focus by exploring a single idea or connected combination of ideas. In Carolyn Forché's 'The Colonel' the poem begins by showing how violence insinuates itself into the everyday in El Salvador, from the pistol lying on a cushion to the construction of the house with broken glass in the walls "to cut a man's hands to lace". Toward the poem's conclusion, when he has emptied a bag of human ears onto the dining table, the colonel remarks dismissively, "Something for your poetry, no?" In a moment of dramatic irony, the colonel could not be more right, as the poem urges the importance of witnessing and reporting abuses of human rights.

Admittedly, 'The Colonel' possesses a number of qualities we see in short-short stories or flash fiction: characters; movement through time; even conflict and hence the suggestion of a narrative arc. Yet the poem's conclusion, with some of the discarded ears hearing the colonel's comment, some of the ears pressing to the ground as though listening for what's coming, suggests that the narrative or story is not the point of the poem, but the vehicle for its central idea, the importance of witness, however meagre the act may seem at times.

What about musicality? As with free verse, prose poems' employment of repetitions of sound varies greatly. At one end of the spectrum, Michael Donaghy's 'Alas, Alice' abounds in both full and partial internal rhyme, assonance, alliteration, and consonance, as the opening sentence, continuing from the title, demonstrates: "who woke to crows and woke up on the ceiling and hung there fearing the evening's sweeping and looked down now at her unfinished reading and loved by sleeping and slept by weeping and called out once.'" The music of Vahni Capildeo's 'Bullshit' is more subtle, with passages of assonance, alliteration, and consonance, as when she describes a group of men as "a warlock pack of Jacks of Clubs." Early in 'The Colonel', Forché uses plosive alliteration to point up the presence of violence amid the domestic: "There were daily papers, pet dogs, a pistol on the cushion beside him."

While free verse can create rhythm through the use of line length and enjambment, prose poetry uses the sentence. 'The Colonel' opens with short, declarative sentences that begin: I was, his wife carried, his daughter filed, there were, the moon swung. The repetition of these short sentences in the same direct, subject-verb construction creates a staccato rhythm that conveys tension. 'Alas, Alice' interweaves excessively long sentences with abruptly short ones, while 'Bullshit' varies sentence length and structure throughout, aptly using sentence fragments to pause and unfold a moment, as at the end of the penultimate stanza-paragraph (which poet and critic Robert Miltner calls 'stanzagraphs'): "He dumps as he goes. The asphalt doubly steaming." Thus the prose poet employs various sentence structures and lengths to influence the pace and rhythm of the poem. The use of various sentence types and lengths is part of the poem's musicality as well as part of its structure.

Seeing how a prose poem works suggests a way into the writing process. If a prose poem creates a concentration or distillation in its focus on a single idea (or, comparably, feeling or mood), then that focus offers a useful starting point for a new poem.

Capildeo's 'Bullshit' seems to begin casually – if we were going to get rid of one word from our language, the poem proposes, my word would be this one. As the poem develops, it becomes clear the figurative use of the word 'bullshit' is the problem, in the way it is used to dismiss others. Thus the poem's central idea is that the speaker would happily see the figurative meaning of bullshit abolished; more broadly, the poem points up how people use language to demean others.

Yet not all prose poems have at their centre ideas as intellectual as Capildeo's and Forché's. Peter Reading's 'Veracruz' evokes the delight in watching thousands of migrating birds, while Hanif Willis-Abdurraqib's 'In Defense of 'Moist'' calls up the many pleasures associated with moisture, whether playing basketball, having sex, or relishing summer weather. Any idea or feeling can become a prose poem's starting point, its origin and focus.

Once a poet has an idea for a prose poem, the question is how to evoke that idea. 'The Colonel' and 'Bullshit' both use narrative, some element of story, as well as imagery. Can anyone who reads 'The Colonel' forget how Forché compares human ears to 'dried peach halves'? While much of the process of drafting a prose poem may be unconscious, it can begin with two questions: what idea or feeling do I want to write about? How can I show or evoke that idea or feeling? A prose poem's conception can be that straightforward.

An intensity of focus

While some go on for pages and pages, usually prose poems best maintain their intensity of focus, the sense of distillation, when they keep to a single A4 page. In my experience, writers generally fall into one of two camps: those who 'spill' or overwrite and then slash away, and those who build a piece of writing word by word. Those who belong to the first camp may, in drafting a prose poem, pursue their idea until they feel

44

they've exhausted it, then begin the editing process by cutting away anything that doesn't relate to that idea or contribute to its evocation. Those who compose word by word may, like me, tend toward prose poems of a single, taut paragraph and do less cutting, more rewriting as they revise.

The use of stanzas or stanzagraphs in prose poetry varies widely. Capildeo's 'Bullshit' employs stanzas in a lyric structure, with each stanza focusing on a particular element in the development of the central idea. The first stanzagraph considers what it would mean to remove a word from our lexicon, the second and third present the speaker's choice of a word to remove and the reason for that choice, and the fourth and fifth evoke the literal use of the word and imply that the speaker wishes that the figurative use had never developed. By contrast, Forché's 'The Colonel' uses a single long paragraph, intensifying the focus, not allowing for a single pause or opportunity to look away. While the handling of stanzas in the prose poem may seem more nebulous than in free verse, often their use comes down to a question of movement or development: do you want to show a development in, or different elements of your central idea and hence employ multiple stanzas, or do you want to hone in on that idea with a tight focus using a single stanza? The more widely we read prose poetry – from Russell Edson to Rosmarie Waldrop to Claudia Rankine to Gary Young – the more we appreciate finer nuances of its stanza use and indeed of all its elements.

Elaborate, investigate, circle, inhabit

The defining characteristics of the prose poem not only give insight in how to compose, but also how to revise one. If the piece elaborates, investigates, circles, or inhabits a single idea or feeling (choose the verb you find most useful), then the first question about the poem's effectiveness is: how well does the poem convey this idea? Is there anything in the poem that detracts from it (and so needs deleting)? What can be done to convey this idea more powerfully?

The second step in revision might then be to consider the poem's musicality. Where would different yet still accurate word choices afford more repetitions of sound, and would that enhance the meaning as well as the music of the poem? Remember Capildeo's "a warlock pack of Jacks of Clubs": all the hard C sounds convey the harshness, the abrasiveness of the speaker's encounter, and hence the strength of the speaker's emotion when the men call her answers 'bullshit.' Similarly, the long O sounds in Donaghy's 'Alas, Alice' suggest a mournful tone before we reach 'weeping.'

When considering a prose poem's musicality in the course of revision, sentence length, and structure become crucial. If I want to heighten tension, as in 'The Colonel,' I might use a succession of short, declarative sentences (though usually not for the entire poem). If I want to create something more languid, I might employ unusually long sentences. For a prose poem that is essentially fluent, I will strive for variety in both sentence structure and length.

Abandoned potential

Definition, composition, revision: what more do we as poets need to know about prose poems? Often the desire to express ourselves in writing is only satisfied if we can find the right vehicle; perhaps for an obsessive poem we employ a pantoum, sestina, or villanelle and find the form's inherent repetition appropriate. Sometimes when we begin a poem in lines, the poem fails to develop beyond one or two short stanzas, and we abandon the poem, unable to see how to complete it effectively. I think many of these abandoned lined poems are prose poems in waiting.

While a prose poem circles a single idea, a lined poem, by virtue of its form, requires some sense of progression or trajectory. When we have an initial idea and can't find any way to develop it beyond that starting point, the poem in lines often stops, aborted. Here is where the prose poem can step in, taking the initial idea, and rather than trying to use it as a starting point, focus on that idea as the *whole point*. Over the years, many students have returned to old, rejected lined poems and fulfilled them by taking the original idea into prose and exploring it for the course of the poem.

Consequently, one of the benefits of reading and writing prose poetry has been that, when I want to pursue an idea in poetry, I am that much more likely to have an effective vehicle – the appropriate form – in which to pursue it. For years, when students have asked me how I contend with writers' block, I have shrugged my shoulders. 'Writers' block?' I say. 'I haven't experienced that in years.' Sometimes I explain that one of the great powers against writers' block – for me – is prose poetry.

Works cited

Venus as a Bear – Vahni Capildeo, (Carcanet, 2018); also available at: https://tankmagazine.com/tank/2018/09/vahni-capildeo/

Conjure – Michael Donaghy, (Picador, 2000).

The Country Between Us – Carolyn Forché, (Harper, 1981); also available at: https://www.poetryfoundation.org/poems/49862/the-colonel.

Robert Miltner, 'Blockheads and Stanzagraphers' from *The Rose Metal Press Field Guide to Prose Poetry* (Rose Metal Press, 2010), pp104-111, eds. Gary L. McDowell and F. Daniel Rzicznek.

Ob – Peter Reading (Bloodaxe Books, 1999).

'In Defense of 'Moist' – Hanif Willis-Abdurraqib, available at: https://westernbeefs.com/abdurraqib/03

A Necklace of Disparate Pearls: On the Ghazal

Debjani Chatterjee

Over several centuries, the ghazal (pronounced 'guzzle') has captured poets' imaginations in many languages. It presents a fascinating combination of strict adherence to form while remaining malleable. This, plus exotic-sounding conventions, has produced an aura of mystery and complexity, but these apparent contradictions can be explained by studying its continuing evolution and expansion into different cultures and languages.

As an undergraduate at the American University in Cairo, I took a module on 'Classical Arabic Literature in Translation'. There I discovered the *qasidah* – a laudatory, elegiac, or satiric ode. I was charmed by the beauty and mood-setting of the *nasib*, the *qasidah's* introductory section, which evolved into an independent poetic form – the ghazal.

Although my studies were mainly in English Language Literature, I had translated some of Nazrul Islam's poems from my Bengali mother tongue. Nazrul was among the first to write ghazals in Bengali, influenced by the songs of his older contemporary Atul Prasad Sen, who had pioneered the Bengali ghazal.

In the 1990s in England, I joined Pakistani British poet Basir Sultan Kazmi, Shropshire poet Simon Fletcher, and Anglo-Irish poet Brian D'Arcy, in creating our multicultural group – Mini Mushaira (*mushaira* is Arabic for 'a poets' gathering'). Basir introduced me to his own fine Urdu ghazals, and those of his celebrated father Nasir Kazmi. Translating their poetry was a privilege. The resulting book was *Generations of Ghazals: Ghazals by Nasir Kazmi and Basir Sultan Kazmi* (Redbeck Press).

Very soon, Brian, Simon and I were writing ghazals in English. From the 1990s onward, we led workshops throughout Britain, spreading our enthusiasm and encouraging others to join in creating ghazals.

Ghazal is an Arabic word that opens many opportunities: *ğazal* or *ğazila* means 'to flirt and engage in flirtatious talk' or 'talking to women' or 'to talk of boys and girls'; *ğazaal* meaning 'a doe or young deer', connects to 'gazelle' in English; *ğazala* means 'to spin (cotton)'; and *ghazal* means 'the cry of a stricken deer'. Whichever meaning one favours, the ghazal is a romantic ode, often expressing yearning. In the Ummayad and early Abbasid periods, ghazals were short, romantic, light musical entertainment. Themes were: `udharî* (courtly love), *hissî* (erotic), *mudhakkar* (homoerotic), and *tamhîdî* (introductory) – also called *taqlîdî* (traditional). `Udharî* ghazals were of longing for an unobtainable beloved – later a major theme in Persian and Indian ghazals. *Tamhîdî* ghazals, also called *taqlîdî*, were 'introductory' because they preceded poetry in another genre, and 'traditional' because they enacted the role of the *nasib*, from which the ghazal evolved.

The ghazal's origins lie in pre-Islamic Arabic *qasidahs*, but it blossomed in the Ummayyad period (661-750) and retained its eminence and continued developing in the early Abbasid period (750-1258), 'the Golden Age of Islam'. As Muslim influence spread Arabic language and culture to Asia, North Africa, and Spain, the ghazal migrated to new lands and languages.

During the Ummayad caliphate, Arabs began their conquest of the Iberian Peninsula. *Al-Andalus*, Muslim Spain, briefly became a great centre of learning and trade, and Cordoba Europe's most cultured city. Europe has known the ghazal since at least the 11th century when it was written in Spain in Hebrew and in Arabic. Two of Spain's greatest poets wrote ghazals: Moses ibn Ezra in Hebrew; and Federico Garcia

Lorca claimed his Arab-Andalusian heritage through ghazals and *qasidahs* in his *Divan del Tamarit*. Nineteenth century Orientalism re-introduced the ghazal to Europe through translations of Persian poetry. Goethe translated ghazals, and wrote his Orient-inspired *West-Eastern Divan*.

The Abbasid period Persians experimented with ghazals in Arabic and Farsi, and by the mid-8th century the Persian ghazal was a distinctive form that attracted the best poets. Two important changes were established in Farsi: the insertion of the *takhallus* or poet's pseudonym in the ghazal's final couplet, and a shift towards autonomous couplets.

Thirteenth century poets like Farid al-Din `Attar and Jalal al-Din Rumi, established the *radif* (refrain) as an embellishment. Attar wrote half his *Divan* or collection with the *radif* after a rhyme, but his younger contemporary Rumi employed it throughout his *Divan-e Shams*.

Many great Persian ghazal poets were Sufis, most famously Saadi Shirazi and Jalaluddin Rumi in the 13th, and Hafiz Shirazi in the 14th centuries. A rich dimension of spirituality, mysticism and philosophy was added to the ghazal's romantic themes and imagery; the Beloved was a metaphor for God, the cup-bearer was the spiritual guide, and wine divine intoxication.

The 13th century Mongol invasion of Central Asia and Iran displaced many poets, scholars and Sufis, who migrated to India. Delhi grew increasingly cosmopolitan. Amir Khusrau, born of a Turkish father and Indian mother, became the first great Indian to write wonderful ghazals in Farsi and Hindavi (Hindustani), a language from which Hindi and Urdu have evolved. His influential Hindavi ghazals reflected a composite Indian culture, while his Farsi ghazals influenced poets down the ages in Farsi-speaking countries, including the great Persian poet Hafiz.

Though it lost status under the British Raj, Farsi continued as a literary language in India until the 20th century; Iqbal (1877-1938) was its last great poet. Even he turned increasingly to Urdu in his last years. Hindavi, then Urdu and Hindi, became Farsi's successor languages in India. But, as Khusrau observed in *Nuh Sipihr* ('Nine Heavens'), every Indian region also had its language: Sindhi, Kashmiri, Gujarati, and so on – these too embraced the ghazal, as have poets writing in English such as Judith Wright, Adrienne Rich and Jim Harrison.

How to explain the attraction? A comment on the Goodreads website does so very well: "It is not 'just' couplets with a repeated ending, a mid-line rhyme – a necklace of disparate pearls held together by a common thread, but a way to speak to universal truths, ending with a reference to the author."

A bewilderingly disjointed sense of unity

The American poet John Hollander famously wrote a ghazal called 'Ghazal' to explain the form. It begins:

> For couplets, the ghazal is prime; at the end
> Of each one's a refrain like a chime: "at the end."

> But in subsequent couplets throughout the whole poem,
> It's this second line only will rhyme at the end.

The features of today's ghazal in English are:
1. *Sher*: Each couplet is a *sher* and can stand independently. *Shers* connect in tone or in theme. Ghazals usually have seven to twelve *shers* (five minimum and fourteen maximum).
2. *Matlaa*: This is the first *sher*. Both lines have the rhyme (*qaafiyaa*) followed by the refrain (*radif*). Each *sher* follows the tone, rhyming pattern and *radif* set by the *matlaa*.
3. *Radif*: This is the refrain. It may be a word or a phrase that ends each line of the *matlaa* and the second line of every *sher* that follows. The rhyming pattern is AA, BA, CA ....

4. *Qaafiyaa*: This is the ghazal's rhyming pattern and is placed immediately before the *radif*.
5. *Maqtaa*: This is the final *sher* and normally contains the *takhallus* or poet's name or pen name in its first or second line.
6. *Takhallus*: The literal meaning is 'to be liberated or to become secure'. This is the poet's actual or pen name. Thus, 'Faiz' was the *takhallus* of Faiz Ahmed Faiz, and 'Ghalib' and 'Asad' were both the *takhallus* of Mirza Asadullah Baig Khan. Sometimes the *takhallus* has a geographical addition to denote where the poet resides, e.g. Daagh Dehlvi meaning 'Daagh of Delhi'. While it is customary to include the *takhallus*, not every *maqtaa* has one.
7. *Beher*: This is the metre in a *sher*. The *matlaa*'s first line establishes the *beher* to be used throughout the ghazal.

That each couplet can stand alone as a poem, enables each *sher* to present a different mood and theme, and is ideal for short performances in *mushairas*. This can also initially make a ghazal seem bewilderingly disjointed – but the uniform metre, similar line lengths, conventions of imagery, strict internal rhyming, and the patterning of language promote an overall sense of unity.

Poets like Agha Shahid Ali, grounded in the subcontinent's ghazal traditions, insist that the ghazal in English follow strict structural rules. In a 1990s interview Ali said, "The form has really been utterly misunderstood in America, with these free verse ghazals. I mean, that's just not the ghazal." But others have argued that English is very different from Indic languages, and poets in English should not be constrained to accept all the 'rigidities' of the ghazal. The same poets would argue that, English being very different from Japanese, an English haiku need only be a very brief poem unfettered by rules requiring three lines with a prescribed number of syllables in each.

Many contemporary ghazal poets in English maintain a syllabic regularity instead of a single uniform metre. Occasionally, poets and translators in English have used tercets and quatrains instead of couplets. A change, increasingly accepted, pertains to the title. Traditionally ghazals do not have titles, but untitled poems are an oddity in English, so many ghazal poets do provide them.

The *takhallus* can be problematic too. Poets in English often feel uncomfortable to give their name within the ghazal, even as a *nom de plume*. Some English language poets like Wright have compromised by giving a name, though not the poet's name.

Rhyme in a ghazal is particularly difficult to maintain since English, unlike Farsi and various Indic languages, has a paucity of rhymes. Some contemporary poets, therefore, employ occasional rhymes, half-rhymes, or omit rhymes; maintaining that the resultant poem is still a ghazal if it preserves other ghazal features. In Mini Mushaira, my colleagues and I prefer the term 'ghazal adaptations' for such compromises.

Below is my example of a ghazal in English, with the *qaafiyaa* italicised and *radif* underlined.

I'm at the End of my Tether

There's too much on my *plate*: I'm at the end of my tether.
It's my unlucky *fate*; I'm at the end of my tether.

Lord, magnify my virtues and overlook my vices.
I am a *reprobate*. I'm at the end of my tether.

You who saved two thieves on Calgary's hill, and forgave all,
Incinerate my *hate*. I'm at the end of my tether.

You threw out the moneychangers and thus cleansed the Temple.
Lord, be my *advocate*; I'm at the end of my tether.

An avatar, you came to fulfill a long made promise.
Guide me to Heaven's *gate*. <u>I'm at the end of my tether.</u>

You struggled with Satan, fought Ravana, vanquished Mara.
You are God *incarnate*. <u>I'm at the end of my tether.</u>

Manifold are your blessed names and beautiful each form.
Teach me to *meditate*. <u>I'm at the end of my tether.</u>

Sudama and the cowherd boys and gopis were your friends.
My dear one, my best *mate*, <u>I'm at the end of my tether.</u>

You once stamped your dance on kingly Kalia's spreaded hood.
Don't say I am too *late*. <u>I'm at the end of my tether.</u>

You who raised Goverdhan in protection, be my shelter.
Debjani cannot *wait*. <u>She's at the end of her tether.</u>

The ghazal adaptation below omits the *qaafiyaa*. The *takhallus* is
substituted by two other names:

Enterprising Harmony

(a Star Trek ghazal)

Science Officer, Mr Spock, raises pointed hand and brow,
and in his usual fashion says: "Live long and prosper."

I am James T. Kirk, Star Trek Captain of the Enterprise;
united, my universal crew live long and prosper.

But Mr Spock is always showing off, upstaging me.
The last thing I want for him is to live long and prosper.

He's a pointy-eared Vulcan imp while I'm only human,
and drama needs conflict – so we can't live long and prosper.

On the other hand, our ratings call for happy endings;
so, for better or worse, Spock and Kirk live long and prosper.

In 'An 'Indian Summer'', I take liberties with the *radif*, using two *radifs* alternating for variation.

An 'Indian Summer'

September – and I see the urban fisher-folk
dreaming of salmon leaping in roaring rivers.

Sunday in Sheffield – and I walk by the canal.
The high Himalayas drum with roaring rivers.

The dragonfly flits in the Yorkshire afternoon
while Mandakini descends in roaring waters.

Once a laughing goddess roamed along these banks;
now unknown, her name resounds through roaring waters.

Ducks swim, ruffling their feathers over this landscape.
Yards away, industry storms its roaring waters.

Whatever she is called, Ganga meditates
on Summer rippling the calm of English rivers.

Note: Mandakini is the Ganges when it flows in Heaven. Many English
rivers were worshipped as goddesses in pre-Christian times.

The ghazal in English is still evolving, with debates swirling
about whether it is a form defined by its structure or its romantic
longings. But it is only by writing them that we as poets shall
settle those debates, if we ever can.

Further reading and listening

Generations of Ghazals: Ghazals by Nasir Kazmi & Basir Sultan Kazmi edited by Debjani Chatterjee (Redbeck Press, 2003).

'Poets of the Ghazal' – podcast in the RLF's 'Writers Aloud' audio series on 21.07.2016 at https://www.rlf.org.uk/showcase/wa_ episode77/

'An Introduction to the Ghazal' by Debjani Chatterjee at https://www.brunel.ac.uk/.../Debjani-Chatterjee-An-Introduction-to-the-Ghazal.pdf · PDF file

In the Bazaar of Love: the Selected Poetry of Amir Khusrau translated by Paul Losensky & Sunil Sharma (Penguin Books India, 2011).

Ravishing DisUnities: Real Ghazals in English by Agha Shahid Ali (Wesleyan University Press, 2000).

Ghazals: Homage to Ghalib by Adrienne Rich (Leaflets, 1968).

The Meanest Flower by Mimi Khalvati (Carcanet, 2007).

Hazaaron Khwahishein Aisi: The Wonderful World of Urdu Ghazals, edited and translated by Anisur Rahman (HarperCollins India, 2018).

The Ghazal Page, e-zine founded by Gene Doty, edited by Holly Jensen in 2015-2016 and by Matt Warren from 2016.

Writing Poems Can Be Real Cool:
On the Golden Shovel

Peter Kahn

Poetic forms can liberate or constrict writers. I've found that forms that carry the weight of history, like sestinas, sonnets and villanelles, can sometimes be intimidating. These forms risk shutting writers down before they even start, or make them try to stiffly imitate the masters, most of whom died long before they were born. I'm not suggesting that we don't try these forms, but I've found a new form – the golden shovel – that provides an entry-way to form which is often more accessible and inviting. It promotes creativity, while providing scaffolding by borrowing words and ideas from another writer. My *Golden Shovel Anthology* co-editor Ravi Shankar calls it the "21st century sonnet".

The golden shovel form was created by National Book Award winner and former *New York Times* poetry editor Terrance Hayes. 'The Golden Shovel (after Gwendolyn Brooks)' appears in Hayes's 2010 collection *Lighthead*. In his foreword to *The Golden Shovel Anthology: New Poems Honoring Gwendolyn Brooks*, Hayes explains how the form came about – as a result of introducing his five-year-old son to poetry via Brooks' 'We Real Cool'. The words and ideas of the poem resonated with Hayes and led to his borrowing all 24 words of the short poem to create his own two-part 48 line poem; he runs each word from 'We Real Cool' vertically down the right margin, as the end words of each line of his new poem.

Gwendolyn Brooks was the first black person to win the Pulitzer Prize in Literature, which she was awarded for poetry, in 1950. She was known for her fierceness, kindness, integrity, community-mindedness, and mentorship. Hayes, who has been awarded a MacArthur Foundation 'genius' grant, is known for experimentation and expanding how poetry can operate. I believe it's in part because he loves challenging himself. Like Brooks, he's known for being kind and giving, among other traits they share. He has been one of my mentors.

I'm often asked for my 'go-to' lesson to help show reluctant writers that they can indeed write a 'good' poem. The golden shovel form is that lesson. I've taught it to thousands of people in the US and the UK, from young people to retirees, from those new to writing to established veterans.

Striking lines

I first recommend reading several Brooks poems, including 'We Real Cool'; *Blacks* is her most comprehensive collection. The Poetry Foundation[6] also has a terrific selection.

After familiarising oneself with Brooks' work I suggest reading Hayes's original golden shovel poem in *Lighthead*. (The poem is also on the Poetry Foundation website.) Finally, I recommend looking at *The Golden Shovel Anthology* to get a sense of the form and the various and varied directions it can lead writers. The anthology contains new work from the likes of Rita Dove, Sharon Olds, Billy Collins, George Szirtes, Patience Agbabi, John Burnside, Nikki Giovanni, Nick Makoha, Roger Robinson, Malika Booker, Inua Ellams, Danez Smith, Raymond Antrobus, Andrew Motion, Nikki Grimes, Jacob Polley, Richard Powers, Mark Doty, Tracy K. Smith and Philip Levine, alongside over a dozen writers who were students at the time of submission, plus in the second edition, eight new poems by student poetry-competition winners.

The initial step for writing a golden shovel poem is choosing a

---

6   www.poetryfoundation.org; Whilst you're there check out an amazing video iteration of 'We Real Cool' created by Manual Cinema in association with Crescendo Literary, with story by Eve Ewing and Nate Marshall and music by Jamila Woods and Ayanna Woods.

'striking line' (or an entire poem) that resonates for one reason or another. This line can come from a Gwendolyn Brooks poem, a song lyric, a novel – any piece of writing.

Mostly the theme or narrative of the work one borrows from provides the context you might need. It could be what the striking line, or even a single word, evokes. If you draw a blank, look for the most evocative words from your borrowed line and try to come up with a story to drive the poem forward. For instance, in the stunning line from Brooks' 'The Children of the Poor', "Lost softness softly makes a trap for us", I am drawn to the words 'lost' and 'trap'. They make me think about times I've literally or figuratively been lost, or about times I've felt trapped, or felt like I trapped someone else.

What I've consistently found is that the golden shovel allows for the imagination to take over in more profound ways than other formal constructs (or even free verse) permit. By drawing inspiration from other writers to use as scaffolding, writers typically avoid the initial stage of writer's block. The borrowed words and the ideas behind them act as a muse, calling forth poems that don't have to be thought out in advance. The form truly challenges one to borrow, or 'sample', in order to create something brand new. This usually leads the writer to surprising places.

In his *Golden Shovel Anthology* poem, Ted Hughes Award winner Raymond Antrobus uses the fragment "each body has its art" from Brooks' 'Gay Chaps at the Bar'. Antrobus says:

> The line "each body has its art" is the opening line of the second poem from the sonnet series "Gay Chaps at the Bar", called "still do I keep my look, my identity…"

> I write golden shovels fast, rarely going over them. There are a number of golden shovels where I initially think, "yes, this is something" and I labour over it, then lose something that felt like a kind of magic. I overthought it. Some lines/ideas

have been lifted directly from my golden shovel into other poems. My poem in the *Golden Shovel Anthology* even built on the following line which isn't included in my poem – "each body has its precious prescribed pose" – the energy of that idea seeped into my poem.

This approach was actually inspired by an 11-year-old student, struggling with her literacy. For her, if I built up her confidence and she wrote fast, her results were so much more interesting and powerful, so I hoped the same would be true for me. I think that's what's amazing about this as a form: it gives you a cage with enough room to put the animal in it.

An addictive playfulness

I recently led a golden shovel workshop for educators from all around the United States. One woman from Ohio shared how she chose a lyric from her wedding song as it had such sentimental value. Her poem was about missing her two-year-old son, as the workshop in Chicago was the first time she'd ever been without him.

It's a form that allows for additional challenges. For instance, Major Jackson's *Golden Shovel Anthology* poem has a Brooks line running down the right margin and a Robert Hayden line running down the left margin. He pays tribute to the first two black National Poet Laureates of the United States in a single poem. In A. Van Jordan's first stanza, he runs his borrowed line down the right margin in the order it appears. For his second stanza, he runs it in reverse order (ie "people who have no children can be hard" followed by "hard be can children no have who people").*Golden Shovel Anthology* co-editor Patricia Smith's poem runs Brooks' 'The Last Quatrain of the Ballad of Emmett Till' down the right margin *and* up the left margin.

Hayes also gives us permission to bend the rules of the form in playful ways. In the original golden shovel poem, he expands the form through hyphenation and the use of imbedded words; he ends a line with the word "ethereal" to allow the borrowed word "real" to be utilised for the form, while allowing a completely different word to be utilised for the context of his poem. Meanwhile, Young Peoples' Laureate for London Theresa Lola included a 'remixed golden shovel' in her collection *In Search of Equilibrium*, where she borrows from Sylvia Plath. Spoken word educator and Chicago-based rapper Adam Levin's '2nd Generation' golden shovel poem below illustrates how one can play with the form:

> *After Kyle Dargan, After Gwendolyn Brooks*
> (Borrowing a line from Kyle Dargan's *Golden Shovel Anthology* poem 'Sustenance': "were the choice mine before beauty what")
>
> When I was a kid, I wasn't afraid of were-
> wolves—but Hannibal "The Cannibal" Lecter always shook me from the
> sheets onto the floor of my bedroom. One night, my father shamed me for
>   my choice
> of fear, told me I should be scared of dictators and their mine-
> fields instead. And suddenly, the world was somehow less and more scary
>   than before.
> In 2017, I miss my old nightmares, and their simple beauty
> Now, my biggest fear is "when" something scary will happen instead
>   of "what."

Levin hyphenates two words, 'were-wolf' and 'mine-field', so that they work vertically to stay true to Dargan's words, while working horizontally in the context of Levin's poem.

Read, relish, borrow, fill, honour

Here's a five-step plan to start writing your own golden shovels:

1. Read
- Read poems by Brooks.
- Read poems by golden shovel creator Terrance Hayes.
- Read poems by my *Golden Shovel Anthology* co-editors, Ravi Shankar and Patricia Smith.

- Read from over 300 Golden Shovel poems in *The Golden Shovel Anthology.*
- Read poems from pretty much anyone.
- Read any other form of literature.
- Peruse through famous quotations.
- Keep an eye out for poetry within prose in newspaper articles and headlines or blog posts.
- Read lyrics from your favorite songs.

2. Relish

- Make note of 'striking lines' or passages in whatever you're reading. In other words, note what pops out as musical, thought provoking, clever or stirring.
- Consider choosing a striking line where the first word is 'strong', that is to say a noun or a verb (such as 'marbles' or 'lurk') as opposed to a preposition, conjunction, adjective or adverb (such as 'and', 'the', 'I' or 'a').
- You may adjust accordingly: if you borrow the line, "I lurched forward and stumbled down the stone path," the first line of your poem could end with 'lurched' rather than 'I'. A 'line' can be loosely defined, as seen in Antrobus's example.

3. Borrow

- Run the borrowed words from the striking line down the right-hand margin of a piece of notebook paper. Using a lined piece of paper will help for your first draft.

4. Fill

- Now fill in the poem, integrating the borrowed words. See where your imagination and creativity takes you. It's up to you whether to take inspiration from the topic or theme of the poem you borrow from. The borrowed words will end each line, but do not have to end each sentence or thought. Remember, you may play around with the words to fit what you're trying to say.

- If you run out of room within your poem, consider adding another striking line from the same author – or from another author. If it's the latter, the poem could be *after Gwendolyn Brooks and Joni Mitchell*.
- When editing your poem, consider adding or removing words within lines for more equal line lengths so that your poem is symmetrical and pleasing to the eye.

5. Honour
- Under your title, always include 'inspired by' or 'after' to honour and bring other readers to the author from whom you borrowed.

I hope the golden shovel provides you with a new form for your poems, as well as introducing you to the work of the remarkable, but often underappreciated, Gwendolyn Brooks.

Let Me Try On Your Tool Belt: On Borrowing Techniques From Short Stories

Tania Hershman

Where to start? There's always "Once upon a time..." Or: "A short story writer and a poet walk into a bar", although that sounds more like a joke. One of my favourite ever short stories begins with "And then...", assuming we already know what precedes those opening words, that there is a relationship, a history. Shall we start there?

And then the short story writer entered with her tool belt. The poet laughed. What on earth is all that for? said the poet.

Poets have tool belts. In the pockets and pouches are marvellous words such as enjambment, rhyme, form, metre, feet, caesuras, iambs, anapests and spondees. When I first began writing poetry six years ago, I was afraid of these terms. As a short story writer, I worried I would be tested on the trochee, questioned on my opinion on enjambment. But I discovered that, firstly, other poets are kinder and less interrogatory than I'd feared. And that to write poetry you don't need to heft this tool belt, you don't need to have studied the concepts. You need to read – but that's true of all writing. The tools are there if you'd like to use them.

What I am here to do, as our short story writer sits down opposite the poet – both of which may be me, yes – is give poets permission to peek into the short story writer's tool belt, pick out a tool or two, feel the weight of it, turn it around, open and close it, and see how it can alter their poem.

Make me a cup of tea, says the short story writer to the poet, and I'll show you what this does. She reaches into a pocket of the tool belt. The poet can see something silver, shiny. The poet turns the kettle on.

Tool 1: Making things up

After fifteen or so years of writing, publishing and teaching short stories, what made me the most nervous about starting to write poetry was that I would never actually write A Poem, that people would point and laugh and say, "That's just a short story with line breaks, you fool!" But I learned – after falling in love with the line and seeing what it could do differently from a sentence that reaches the right margin – is that a poem can also be a story, just as a short story, especially flash fiction, the shortest of short stories, can also be a poem. And the first and greatest tool short story writers have is: fiction.

Short story writers are big liars. We love doing it, we are always making up people, inventing places, writing about situations we have never been in, planets we have never travelled to at warp speed through a wormhole. Yes, some of the greatest short stories may be what we call 'thinly-veiled autobiography', but the point is that when you wave your fiction wand over your words, no-one will ever know. You have licence to do whatever you want.

Real life doesn't often make for a great short story, doesn't always have enough of what I call 'what-happened-nextness' to grip a reader and keep them reading. A story has certain needs. Poets also want to keep a reader's attention, whether it's for ten lines or ten pages. Fiction can be a way to approach a topic, a dilemma, a scenario that you don't want to look at directly. Fictionalising can help you approach it from the side instead of head on.

Also: theft. Fiction writers are magpies, and I do this as a poet too. One of my poems is about someone else's father taking apart a clock, an anecdote the son told us all at a conference I went to. That would be a great poem, I thought. So I took it.

How can I believe anything you're telling me? said the poet, blowing on her tea.

Ah, said the short story writer, grinning. Who knows if I'm not an unreliable narrator? Only time will tell.

Tools 2, 3, 4, 5: Character, Point of view, Voice, Dialogue

The next greatest tool in the short story writer's belt is character. A short story stands or falls on how compelling the main character is, how much we can hear his voice, feel that she leaps off the page, that they are real. Because if they seem real, we care about them and want to know what they do in response to whatever fiendish situation the writer has placed them in.

When I tiptoed into the world of poetry, one of the first things I noticed in workshops – as a participant and, more recently, as a teacher – is how little anyone talked about character, how most poems have the *feel* of autobiography and are told in the first-person voice. I understand that: poetry has allowed me, for the first time, to directly use events from my life. But I also feel free, with a background in fiction, to write these poems from someone else's point of view, to give the experiences to a character in order to get a little distance from me, which makes me more comfortable getting it down on the page. When I was writing about my own anxieties in social situations, for example, I wrote: "She does not expect/ to be recognised/ from one occasion to the next", because to write "I do not expect..." was too much for me. I couldn't do it.

There are a number of tools for this – the character can be male, female, or anything else, from a chicken to a chair. Then there's voice: what words does your character use, what is her particular language, in her head or to other people? What words or phrases does he use, what dialect, what rhythms?

Which brings us to another tool: dialogue is incredibly useful in short stories not only to let us hear a character's voice, but to get across a great deal about a situation without having to stop and explain. Let the characters in your poem talk to each other – and when you are out in the world, listen to how people really speak, how rare it is that someone says exactly what they mean, or answers anyone directly. Conversations are as much about what is not said as what is spoken.

And: point of view. You can still use first person:

> I showed the poet my tool belt

or play around:

> She let the poet try on her tool belt
> You showed the poet what was inside one of your pockets
> We let the poet use our favourite tool

I have a particular fondness for the last two, second person and first person plural, I like the atmosphere they create. Try one, see how it feels. Then try another.

What about me? says the narrator, who is sitting in a corner, watching the short story writer and the poet drink tea.

The narrator is one of the short story writer's favourite people. The narrator watches whats's going on, can sometimes dip inside characters' heads to read their thoughts, and not only knows more than each one character, but might know the future too. Although some narrators are unreliable, you never really know if you can trust what they're telling you. They're the most fun.

Tools 6, 7: Tenses, Time

When is all this happening? the poet will ask. The short story writer will refuse to answer; she has taken down the kitchen clock and neither of them will be wearing watches.

As well as lying, sometimes spectacularly, short story writers love to travel in time. A short story might stretch an hour over ten pages, or compress a year into a paragraph. In that white space between sections, a decade might have passed. The story may be told in the present tense, says the short story writer to the poet; the past tense has worked well, the poet answered, or even the future tense, as above. Different tenses create different atmospheres: the present tense doesn't allow you to settle, it gives you the feeling, as a reader, that you and the writer are experiencing this together, neither of you knowing what might come next. The past tense is less edge-of-seat stuff, more a recording of what occurred, a testimonial, a remembrance.

In one of the tool belt's pouches you'll find the flashback and the flashforward, a two-headed tool. Slip back to show us something that happened yesterday or a hundred years ago – or skip forwards to see what will happen as a result of this day, this hour. My 16-line poem 'And What We Know About Time' (remember the anecdote from the conference?) begins in childhood, then takes us forward ten years, and the ending brings us to now. There's a lot you can do with time, even in a very small space.

The poet and the short story writer won't meet again until a party, twenty years later. Do you still have that tool belt, the poet says, kissing the short story writer on the cheek. She blushes, looks around for the nearest waiter with the drinks.

Tools 8, 9: Beginnings and endings: The shape of a story

The only thing a short story has to be is short. A poem, of course, might be book length, or even span several volumes. But a great many poems don't tend to require you to turn the page more than once, if that; and here is the space where the short story, especially flash fiction, and the poem, sitting together, find the most to talk about. Beginnings and endings.

I very rarely make grand pronouncements about anything, but from years and years of reading short stories and amassing data on the kinds of stories I love, that leave me reeling, feeling like I've been punched in the stomach, I say this: you can't have a great short story that doesn't have a great ending. And the same is true for a poem.

Endings are hard. You know when you read a good one, the right mix of stopping before everything is tied up neatly, but not too soon, leaving so much unsaid that a reader is dissatisfied, confused (unless, of course, your aim is to confuse and dissatisfy, which is a risk, but go for it, I say.)

My second pronouncement is that the greatest short stories and poems work because their endings resonate with their beginnings in some way, so where you choose to begin affects where you choose to end. Or rather: once you've got to your ending, you can look back and see if where your draft starts is the right point. I often find with both stories and poems that I have buried the beginning in the middle, because I've had to write my way into it, the way a high-jumper has a run-up before she leaps. So I delete the first paragraph, the first few lines.

With flash fiction and the short poem, both of which tend to be less than a page long, the reader can see the ending out of the corner of his eye, knows that it's coming soon, that she won't be in this world for long. This sets up an expectation about endingness, about transience.

Tool 10, 11: Play, Show don't tell

And as the ending of our time together approaches, I have two last tools. I've had such fun writing this, and that is one: the joy of playing, letting loose, allowing yourself to interrupt an essay with scenes between a short story writer and a poet, in two different fonts. And my final tool is 'Show don't tell', something fiction writers are always banging on about. This means that, instead of saying:

 The poet was broken-hearted, didn't know if she'd ever love again

you show us:

The kettle seemed heavier to her than it had ever been. She gave up on making tea and stood staring at the photos on the fridge.

I hope that's what I've done here, not just to tell you about the tools you might use, but to illustrate what they can do, and give you permission to add them to your own poetic tool belt.

Two days after the party, the poet and the short story writer each receive a parcel containing the identical object, a tool neither of them has ever seen before. The tool comes with a note with only one instruction. "Play", it says.

When Two Become One: On the Coupling, a Poetic Invention and Intervention

Karen McCarthy Woolf

"Poetry is not only dream and vision; it is the skeleton architecture of our lives. It lays the foundations for a future of change, a bridge across our fears of what has never been before." – Audre Lorde, *Poetry is Not a Luxury*

For a long time I thought the reason I wrote poetry was because I was interested in structures: and more specifically architecture. This is true, in that for me making poems is more akin to sculpture than painting. In the contemporary sense, that vessel, that shape, may also play out as installation, as a sensory, kinetic force. The relationships between absence, presence, sound and silence manifest on the page and through other media, which will exact their own formal requirements.

This brings me to a second, never secondary passion: music, which has been a constant, enduring companion throughout my life. Sometimes it's the casual conversation which helps us arrive at a deeper understanding. In the airport security queue, trying to explain what kind of poetry I write to a fellow queue-ee, I finally arrive at something that makes sense. *No, not lyrics, as in lyrics for songs, but lyric, contemporary lyric, by which I mean not writing words to go with music, but trying to write music with words.* It's a musical building, with a finely calibrated soundsystem, a handbuilt speaker stack, a stage, and maybe an orchestra, elevated – not in a pit – and lots of electronica, machines, synths, and unidentified as well as familiar instruments. Always drums. Goat skin ++. Physically more like a teepee. So the poem as nightclub? Yes, but the nightclub as underground, afterhours venue, as mash-up squat party with loos leaking through the roof and scant regard to health &

safety, people smoking *indoors*, with DJs playing all kinds of stuff that blurs categories and genres, and sweat running down the walls. Maybe outside there's a wildflower meadow in the middle of an industrial estate. *So, what, like rap or spoken word?* my airport pal enquires. Yes that could be there, but it's only a possibility, not an absolute. You might hear a little sonnet trill, trill; or something scratchy go bleep or a kora mingle with a vibraphone. It could be disco, electro, techno or funk or jazz.

Yet, when we think of traditional poetic form it is the default edifice that looms, large and imposing, more like the British Museum, maybe the pyramid at the Louvre at best; sounds like Beethoven or Mahler on a Classic FM compilation. It is the last bastion of 'The Gatekeepers', the hoop we must hop, skip and jump through if we are to be taken *seriously*. That said, I *love* form. In *all* its forms. For its astringent properties that can facilitate a significant edit, for its relationship with rhyme, rhythm, song and other particular sonic and socio-cultural endowments. For the historical echoes and geographical landmarks. For the discipline. For the challenge. Landay-sonnet hybrid anyone? Bring it on. There's no harm in trying. Is that a first collection, sweet troubadour? It must be sestina o'clock. Is there a pantoum in that prize-winning pamphlet? I'm being flippant, but only slightly. Form for its own sake is a contorted and pointless gymnastics. It's what we use it for, the nature of the seeds we broadcast that matters. But I think we need to recognise it as a hierarchical creature, remembering along the way that etymologically speaking, *hierarch* has its roots in the idea of sacred rule. As poetic utterance booms to the basement it also reaches up, into the atmosphere. Form is the vehicle that can take us there.

Terrance Hayes is an inventor of a number of new forms, most notably the golden shovel, which he devised to mark Gwendolyn Brooks' centenary (see Peter Kahn's essay, page 57). Brooks was the first black woman to win the Pulitzer Prize for *Annie Allen*, which was published in 1949. I was struck by a quotation in her biography from the critic George E Kent, who said she occupied "a unique position in American letters. Not only has she combined a strong commitment to racial identity and equality with a mastery of poetic techniques, but she has also managed to bridge the gap between the academic poets of her generation in the 1940s and the young black militant writers of the 1960s." Inherent in the observation, complimentary as it appears and was most likely intended, is the idea that the doors of the academy swing open if, and only if, writers of colour observe its accepted architectures of excellence and mastery. And even then, they may not open easily, or in a welcoming manner. In his essay 'Wallace Stevens After Lunch', Major Jackson comments on an anecdotal moment, after a long and boozy lunch meeting of the National Book Award Committee (a fact much-dwelled upon by apologist critique, that booziness), when Stevens, seeing a photo of Brooks on the wall, is said to have asked, 'Who's the coon?'.

It feels fitting therefore that Hayes' shovel, a derivative technique as the name suggests, is an instrument through which its practitioners might enrich and diversify the canon. What it brings with it is an opportunity to reconsider the line break on a granular level (most exemplary is Hayes' original, double shovel, on Brooks' 'We Real Cool'), the possibilities of thematic amplification and a system of referenced allusion that collates a community of voices.

I've written a few shovels; some went the way of other 'exercises' and morphed into something else later down the line. Others survived. What also grew from writing them was a sense of permission. If Hayes could invent a form, why couldn't I?

A form of invention

I didn't really set out to devise a new form when I started though. I was writing a sequence on horse chestnuts after a mature tree in my back garden fell in a storm the day before

Christmas Eve. I loved that tree and the ecosystem it hosted: the animals that lived in it, its shiny brown seeds that fell too early now it was weakened by blight. Although I'd just written a book of elegies (*An Aviary of Small Birds*, Carcanet, 2014), another presented itself to me – this time for nature, and the self-inflicted losses humanity must now endure as a result of climate crisis.

My research took me to Charles Darwin, and specifically the postscript to a letter he wrote to a friend, about the horse chestnut's botanical composition and behaviours. As I looked at the paragraph on my computer screen I began to play around with the lines. There's something in the postscript which is very particular: it's got the language of the letter, which outside of business and legal use is conversational and questioning in feel and tone, yet it is more casual, almost throwaway but often accidentally germane. I'd recently written a poem 'Of August' in which I deprived the text of one of its compositional cornerstones, the image – in a bid to stretch the idea of what a poem could or might be without that default position. I was also thinking about how that might apply to the differences and similarities between lyric and prose, about the lyric essay, and as always, about music. What might happen if you start with an intrinsically prosaic piece of text – ideally out of copyright for publication purposes – something quite flat sonically, and see what it takes to push it towards lyric?

I started to write lines underneath – recalling the oral tradition of call and response. I also devised some 'rules' with the thought of eliciting the lyric behind them. It's a simple enough process:

1. Find a piece of prose. Ideally this will be something 'non-poetic', probably non-fiction.
2. Cut it up into poetic lines. This is probably something you will play around with and shift to suit your purposes.
3. Write a response line underneath so as to continue and shift the narrative arc.
4. The response line should ideally contain rhyme, repetition

or assonance as an echo of the line above so as to create the 'couplet'.

5. Retain the original punctuation if you can (be warned however, it is mind-blowingly fiddly and only recommended for those that really love that kind of conundrum).

6. Ideally you will have two co-existing narratives that combine to read as one.

Taking that original poem, 'Horse Chestnut II', as an example, which you can read in full in my collection *Seasonal Disturbances* (Carcanet, 2017) you can see how the form seeks to both amplify and subvert the original. Here Darwin's lines are in Roman, mine in Italic.

> *P.S.* | As Horse-chesnuts [sic] have male flowers
> *when a man comes into his flowering season*
>
> & hermaphrodite flowers I have wished to examine
> *with petals soft and tender as breasts, open to bare*
>
> their pollen,
> *his seed*
>
> & this has made me observe
> *& this has made me*
>
> a thing which has surprised me. — All the flowers
> *an entreaty, flowering labiatae*
>
> now open on my *several* trees
> *now open and in profusion*
>
> are *male* with rudimentary pistil
> *are female too, rude and raw*
>
> with *pollen shedding*; so that I began to think
> *how dishevelled I was, how*
>
> my memory had deceived me
> *into enamour* […]

I wanted to link the two texts, the old and the new, but also create a fresh narrative. I was also aware of Darwin's voice, as iconic to the stereotypical authority of the white, Victorian male. That he'd used the word "hermaphrodite" invited another level of engagement on gender, so there's this sense of wanting to disrupt and undermine the certainties of that scientific register, as indicated by the idea that a man might have "a flowering season", a conceit that might have been seen as traditionally feminine, particularly in the nineteenth century.

Resisting the binary

The possibilities to expose and resist the binary via the couplet's duality, which can simultaneously rupture and repair, was also compelling. I'd spent many years writing about death, which has been metaphorically synonymous with sex, and climax, so there was an urge to push the poem into a more playful, sensuous territory that capitalises on the botanical lexicon. The assonance of words and phrases such as "rudimentary" and "rude and raw"; "pollen shedding" and "dishevelled"; or "memory" and "enamour" also helped to ramp up the music. It's an asymmetric harmony in that sense; more junglist mash-up as a posthumous duet with the spirit of the sample behind it, rather than anything more quietly melodious. This appeals to me on a mischievious level: that Darwin might, unwittingly, be involved in such an endeavour.

Having grown up in London as an English-Jamaican hybrid I think the impulse to unify seemingly disparate parts is part of a larger poetic. For me, identity doesn't always play out through an explicit thematic articulation; it might express, as I think it does here, through form. The interventionist project plays out quite gently, although it might be something more vigorous and interrogative in character. Malika Booker used the form in a commission for the Manchester Poetry Festival as a means by which to query the composition and content of right-wing political speeches. Finding the appropriate text, in terms of what you might want to write into, or against, may take time and involve a process of rejection and selection. Peter Raynard's *The Combination: A Poetic Coupling of the Communist Manifesto*, published by Culture Matters, brings Marx's political discourse into contemporary focus.

Ideally, a coupling is a poem that can be read as two individual pieces or altogether as one. I wrote another, 'Crossings', for a commission for the Newcastle Poetry Festival, using text from a visual art catalogue written by the post-minimalist abstract painter Sean Scully. There I didn't take the paragraph as a whole, although previously that had been a 'rule', but used a number of sentences from the text strung together. In that piece, the traction is all around the possibilities of 'coupling', as a form of union, and is a homage to that most sacred space: the dancefloor. It can be downloaded as an app called Crossings, and it's a piece I'd like to extend and will collaborate on with an electronica producer, so its form will adopt another, more multi-dimensional shape.

Taking someone else's writing and mutating it to suit your own purpose is interventionist, even revisionist. But there's also an ethic of transparency, in that the original is there, and that its source or author is credited or acknowledged (usually by way of a footnote or an epigraph under the poem title) so the process itself is visible. As such the coupling can also been seen as another form of reading, that requires us to dig in and enter a pre-existing text more deeply in a bid to make something new. Unlike the found poem, it is less passive and more active – it has the capacity to shift or even mangle a perceived meaning, which might then act as a form of literary critique. In the words of Audre Lorde, again, "the masters tools will never demolish the master's house". The coupling is not an entirely new tool, but it's my hope that the form might make its way as a poetic device through which we can resist, interrogate, amend and refresh the canon.

PART TWO

ON MAKING POEMS

The Discipline of Getting Lost: On the Impossibility of Poems

Caroline Bird

Writing a poem is impossible and once you realise this, you're free.

Rimbaud said that the language of poetry is not brain to brain but 'soul to soul' which is, of course, impossible:

> Hands full of sand, I say:
> Take this, this is what I have saved;
> I earned it with my genius,
> and because I love you...
>
> take this, hurry.
> I am dropping everything.
> – James Tate

Yes, a poem is a gift from my soul to yours but I will have dropped most of it on the floor before it reaches you. With each poem, we try to remove the soul from our chests and thrust it through the window of the blank page into the arms of the world – "take this, hurry, I am dropping everything" – but most of it slips through our fingers in transit. Each poem demonstrates the sheer inexhaustible desire we have to communicate the essence of ourselves whilst simultaneously proving this to be impossible. It's like trying to converse with the ocean using only your eyebrows, post a letter into a stranger's forehead, clean a skyscraper with your tongue. Each poem is an attempt to communicate something wordless... using words.

> Ever Tried. Ever Failed. No matter. Try again. Fail again. Fail better. – Samuel Beckett

The impossibility is what keeps us writing; that perpetual

81

hunger, that endless dissatisfaction, trying to smuggle something real across that writer-reader border as we slip through the gaps between our own words.

> The brightness of a new page where everything yet can happen. – Rainer Maria Rilke

First drafts are often assumed to be the undisciplined part, that you just 'write whatever comes into your head' or 'splurge'. I contest this: the first draft is the most disciplined part of all, the hardest part, because you have to stay hyper-awake to the unknown, let the images lead you down the hallways of your imagination, opening doors to rooms you've never entered before. You have to maintain vehement and unfounded faith in a poem that may never exist, and even if it does will never truly voice the heart of your intentions. How glorious is that?

> The blood jet is poetry,
> There is no stopping it.
> – Sylvia Plath

So how do you start an impossible task? I don't know. No, really, the answer is "I don't know". That is how you start. By not knowing. When Wislawa Szymborska accepted the Nobel Prize in Literature, she said in her speech: "Whatever inspiration is, it's born from a continuous I don't know." We have to continually work at not knowing, re-clouding our own eyes, reopening ourselves to discovery, unlearning the world to encounter it afresh. So the next time you click your pen and think "I've got nothing" – correct! That's exactly where you should be starting... that's where the Nobel Prize winners start; with nothing, with the radiant blankness.

> When a poet is willing to risk not-knowing, that's when something might happen. – Chase Twitchell

People talk about the fear of the blank page. Turn this thought upside down – the blankness is the best bit. The blankness is vital, it's the "continuous I don't know" that births the poem, the breath that precedes the words, the thin air from whence something can magically appear. You can't have magic without thin air, and you can't have inspiration (whatever that is), without blankness, and so our first job, in the writing of a poem, is to resist the temptation to thicken our air with pre-empting, to let go of the need for an *outcome*. First drafts are entirely about discovery and you can't plan a surprise. But it's counter-intuitive isn't it? Why would you step forward without the certainty of ground? How do we trust nothingness? Unlearn in order to encounter? And how on earth can 'getting lost' be a discipline?

Fling open the door of your first line

Sylvia Plath once described the experience of reading a poem as "a door opens, a door shuts. In between you have had a glimpse: a garden, a person, a rainstorm, a dragonfly, a heart, a city." If reading a poem is like glimpsing behind a door, then to *write* a poem you must fling open the door, create the world behind it *and* respond to it. Such a complicated imaginative gesture can only be accomplished through rash audacity. Write a first line that thrusts you out, unprepared, into a world of your own making:

> A second New York is being built
> a little West of the old one
> – David Berman

Well, if you write a line like that, you have to finish the poem, don't you? Because now you have a duty to respond. You have flung open the door of the page, giving yourself no choice but to step through. Many first lines work this way:

> Dearest, the cockroaches are having babies
> – Lavinia Greenlaw

> Sofia used pigeon blood on her wedding night
> – Warsan Shire

All of a sudden she began to whistle
  – Mary Oliver

It always starts with a dead girl
  – Jane Yeh

As readers, we often assume the poet wouldn't write an evocative opening without an inkling of where the poem was going. In fact, it's one of the best tricks you can play on yourself to force you out into the nothingness... and that's what first drafts are all about, tricking yourself into believing in the existence of a new poem.

Get disqualified from your own poem

In the middle of the forest there is an unexpected clearing
that can only be found by those who have gotten lost.
  – Tomas Tranströmer

Rev up, don't wrap up. When you reach the line you instinctively suspect is the end (perhaps it neatly sums up an emotion or brings the situation to a close, or lands on a particularly beautiful image) slalom through it, keep going, past the finish line, over the motorway into the forest until you get eaten by a bear or land in a ditch; deliberately overshoot. Even if the first draft descends into total nonsense, even if you're tired and irritated and especially if you have nothing left to write. The best lines arise when you have nothing left. If you continue past the assumed ending of your first draft, a wonderful feeling occurs – freedom. This bit was never even meant to be here! I'm in no-man's land! Whatever I say or do in this place *beyond the poem* has no consequence because no one will ever read it! Of course, later, you might discover your poem actually began the second you crossed that finish line, that the entire 'official' section of your first draft was written by your well-behaved self but then a deeper voice emerged, emboldened by that dark and untamed place beyond the poem...

Believe your images

> Poems are like dreams: in them you put what you don't
> know you know. – Adrienne Rich

Whilst writing, don't ever think about the word 'metaphor'. If you think "I'm writing a metaphor now", then you are instantly entering into a process of translation, trying to tame the image into a fixed job of emotional representation – which immediately stops the poem from feeling alive in your mind. A metaphor doesn't know it's a metaphor, it thinks it's real, just like a dream believes itself, so the poet's job is to dream the dream not translate it. The reader can wake up from the poem later and scratch their head and go "what did that mean?", but if you keep asking yourself "what does this image mean?" as you write, then you are essentially violently waking yourself up over and over and disrupting your own imaginative progress. If you concentrate on visualising the poem's world, writing down what you see like your own mental-scribe, then your feelings will naturally infuse your images (as they do when you sleep) and the metaphorical danger will be greater because your subconscious is the engine room of imagery. You can write images *before* you understand them. The understanding may come later but the first draft is pure hunger; it doesn't care about your logic.

Carry on until the subject matter is no longer what the poem is about

> If you have any idea for a poem, an exact grid of intent,
> you are on the wrong path, a dead-end alley, at the top of
> a cliff you haven't even climbed. – Mary Ruefle

Don't wait for a fully formed idea, get one line, one word – *doppelganger, mushroom, dildo* – and fling your pen at the paper like an animal starved of blood, but then commit with all seriousness to the discovery of feeling, keep writing until the subject matter is no longer what the poem is about. In many ways, it doesn't matter which opening image you choose so long as you choose one. If you commit with enough gusto and grit to following the impetus of language, writing into the nothingness, focusing on the pictures as they appear in your head, then literally any subject matter can and will lead you to profundity whether you like it or not. A poem about a baked bean is suddenly all about your mother dying. A poem about a rusty rat-infested skip is suddenly about the love of your life. As Wayne Holloway Smith said recently, "Lean into any subject matter hard enough, you will leave an imprint of yourself." However, again, you can't pre-empt how or why this will happen; you can't say to yourself "this baked bean will become a metaphor for my mother's death" because that's cheating, and it won't work. You have to honestly not know where it will take you. Each time you perch on the ledge of a blank page, fight the urge to strap on the parachute of a 'meaning'. Let your imagination catch you.

Get out of your own way

> When I make the mistake of imagining how a whole poem
> should unfold, I immediately want to destroy that plan.
> Nothing should supplant the true act of discovery.
> – James Tate

Beware your authorial voice interrupting you with questions like "Where is this going?" "What is this about?" and "Is this even poetry?" Your inner critic will try, with dogged determinedness, to disrupt the momentum of your first draft and this is where the discipline element really comes in. You must continually – and I mean, continually – reject the guidance proffered by your own self-doubt. Your inner critic will approach you with a road-map ("write a poem about this... this is a worthy poetic topic") – burn that map! Slap that compass from their scared and clammy hands. Don't let your insecurity tame your poem and force you back onto a known path, keep knitting from the air.

Hope

> All poetry is a form of hope.
> – Dean Young

I always think about the lines from Leonard Cohen's 'Suzanne': "There are children in the morning/ they are leaning out for love/ and they will lean that way forever." Poets are children in the morning, leaning out forever, and poetry is hope not because of its content but because of the act itself. Even the most miserable, cynical, semi-suicidal poem is still powered by the belief that someone or something – some peopled loneliness on the horizon of the poet's mind – cares enough to be interested in your soul, whatever that is. As Fanny Howe said, "The point of art is to show people that life is worth living by showing that it isn't."

We are all leaning out of the windows of those blank pages, trying to feel the sun on our faces, trying to meet ourselves somehow. We think poetry is about the wonder of words... but it's also about the ineptitude of words: they never work, never fully express, never contain the contents of our hearts, it's all too big, every sentence is a sieve and yet we keep on trying. Failure isn't the risk but the point: each poem falls short so we write another. *"Take this, hurry, I am dropping everything."*

Active Lines and Scoring Goals: On Line Breaks

Moniza Alvi

Paul Klee's first lesson in art from his *Pedagogical Sketchbook* involved "An active line on a walk, moving freely, without a goal." A single line in poetry could also be described as "an active line" carrying, ideally, a sense of the unwilled, of exploration and freedom of movement. In open form (or so-called free verse) the use of the line as an entity with a beginning and ending is particularly valuable in helping to define a poem as a poem. James Longenbach, in his book devoted to the poetic line, argues: "More than metre, more than rhyme, more than images or alliteration or figurative language, line is what distinguishes our experience of poetry as poetry." An excerpt of prose, or a prose poem may contain many of the features of poetry, rhythmic strength, for example, and intricacy of language, but what will surely be missing is the active role played in poetry by the line endings. While prose makes a virtue of the absence of this feature, poetry makes a virtue of its presence.

Idiosyncrasy

To turn first to the original and resourceful twentieth-century poet Stevie Smith. Her flexible use of the poetic line, in combination with her destabilising tonal and vocal shifts, contributes strongly to the dramatic impact of her late poem 'Angel Boley', in which she responds to the 'moors murders', that most notorious series of crimes against children in twentieth-century Britain. Smith focusses on the avenging Angel and a murdering pair, Hark and Malady, Angel's husband and mother. The aspects which make up the fabric of this *tour de force* of a poem – psychological urgency, the fairytale and religious elements, the narrative and its drama – are held together by Smith's innovative use of the line.

Smith creates a fairytale swiftness, line breaks and enjambment carrying tensions, controlling suspense and distributing emphasis in the narrative. At the poem's climax, Smith lingers on the gathering of the mushrooms with which Angel is to poison the murderers:

> As soon as Angel
> Said to herself: I am the Angel of Death
> She became at once very practical and went out into the woods
>   and fields
> And gathered some of A. Phalloides, commonly called the 'white'
>   or deadly
> Amanita, a mushroom of high toxicity. These poisonous fungi
> She put into a soup, and this soup she gave
> To Hark, and her mother, Malady, for supper, so that they died.

At this stage of the poem Smith's line breaks enhance urgency, while the sophistication of this formal feature underlines that this isn't a children's poem but a story told to adults. The slowing of the pace, along with the destabilising shift of voice and tone, marks a departure from the traditional fairytale mode of the poem and makes it impossible to feel comfortable in her text as a reader might in a more conventional telling. The anarchic use to which Angel will put the poisonous mushrooms is reflected in a stylistic technique, in combat with traditional poetry, yet in the service of a strong, idiosyncratic poem. Smith, for example, interrupts the poem's opening stanza with a short line "As soon as Angel", thus emphasising the name 'Angel' and highlighting its symbolic resonance. The second short line ends with "Angel of Death", thus emphasising the name again and that this Angel is, unexpectedly, the 'Angel of Death'. This abrupt change in the poem's voice signals the potent blend of the religious with the fairytale. Smith then immerses the reader, by means of longer enjambed lines, in the busy activity of the gathering of the mushrooms and their identification. In this way she enables the reader to feel, along with Angel, the relish of the prospective poisoning, and to believe, momentarily, in the rightness and necessity of Angel's act of vengeance. Smith achieves strongly here that which Freud (in his study of Michelangelo's statue of Moses), suggests as the artist's aim: "to awaken in us the same emotional attitude, the same mental constellation as that which in him produced the impetus to create."

Darting motion, creating surprise

It seems fitting that Sujata Bhatt, one of the most cosmopolitan of contemporary poets, with a multi-faceted identity (raised in India, educated in the USA, now living in Germany), chooses to write in a fractured, but strongly-cadenced open form. Her striking use of line breaks contributes to the vitality of her poems and their sense of enquiry, allowing her vibrant images to breathe. Consider, for example, her poem 'The Peacock'. The irregular indentation of lines suggests the movement of the bird, the lines themselves following a darting motion and recreating the incident in the present:

> His loud sharp call
> seems to come from nowhere.
> Then, a flash of turquoise
> > in the pipal tree.
> The slender neck arched away from you
> > as he descends,

Each image is imprinted separately on the mind and given a moment to exist. We could imagine the same poem arranged more traditionally, with lines and stanzas of regular length and consider what it would lose in terms of vivacity and individuality. Try the first line as the unbroken "His loud sharp call seems to come from nowhere." We would be deprived of the sense of being able to hear the call because its sound would be muffled by the end of the sentence, and the line would trail limply away. In the poem's second stanza the isolated "I was told" of the opening line highlights the idea of story, and briefly allows us to fantasise a circumstance of the telling. Images are given unexpected emphasis by broken off ends of lines, and the reader is allowed to concentrate on them. Partly through such structuring of her poems, Bhatt's poetry enacts an intense moment-by-moment concentration.

Generally it's important that a line break creates a surprise, however small, before the poem's subsequent line. You wouldn't want to read the opening of a line having anticipated it beforehand. Although line breaks may well have been made unconsciously by the poet, when looking back, it's as well that reasons can be given for them in terms of what they're doing, or achieving, in the poem. Another consideration is that every line, even if very short, needs to be a strong line, sufficiently alive, or energetic. As regards the spacing of the poem on the page, we're often drawn to the slight pause, like a rest in music, the ringing silence that a line ending can provide, along with the visual impact of the space created.

My recent poetry collection *Blackbird, Bye Bye* was inspired by the lives of my parents and the death of my father. Partly to create a sense of my father as an immigrant and my parents locating and relocating in Pakistan and England, I drew on birds allegorically and shaped several of the poems to give an impression of wings or flight. This involved much conscious sculpting of poems and I became more strongly focussed than usual on the line endings and how they might, or might not, work. I had to ensure that the line breaks contributed to a viable shape, and also made sense in terms of the meaning of the poems. It was quite a challenge, but this decision-making did lead to greater, and, I hoped, fruitful experimenting.

In, for example, the long, segmented central poem 'The Afterlife of Fatherbird', where I talk to my father after his death, I tried to suggest flight with stepped lines. The idea was that, in terms of the layout, both the line beginnings and the line endings would be patterned to indicate movement. Here is section 7, for instance, about halfway through the poem:

You knew (perhaps still know) so much about flight –
the long-haul, the slow-looping against
the wind and into the sun, the disentangling.

When to halt and where to settle, when to carry on
and who to choose for company.
At one with your soul, you flew beneath

between and over, East-West, West-East, carved a way
into the unfamiliar, made your own weather –
captain of the flying club for years

until swiftly, acutely, you flew one way

and the world, the other.

Just as Fatherbird was carving his way, I was also carving the poem, playing with its layout and attempting to give some impression of flight. It was particularly enjoyable, by means of enjambment, to carry this flight across stanzas, sometimes, as well as lines. Thus the phrase "beneath // between and over" was broken across the stanza, to accord with the poem's pattern, but also to evoke a continuity of flight. At instances in the poem, I made some stand-alone lines to create space and cadence, as well as to give emphasis. I was also keen to avoid any possible rigidity of form. Perhaps the isolated lines also give the impression of loose feathers! The pattern of longer and shorter lines sometimes took a while to achieve. The challenge was to make the whole poem sound and appear as natural as possible.

Tribute ghosts

A potentially instructive and enjoyable form to try is a 'golden shovel' poem (see Peter Kahn's essay, page 57). In this form, created by the poet Terrance Hayes as a response to the poem by Gwendolyn Brooks, 'We Real Cool: The Pool Players. Seven at the Golden Shovel', the last words of each line are a line, or lines, taken in order from the poem of a chosen poet. This form generally involves some less conventional line endings and often results in a liveliness of rhythm and diction, an experience of playfulness and 'letting go'. One of the satisfying aspects of the form is that the original poem ghosts behind the new one which acts as a tribute to it. The challenge is to create a poem that benefits from less conventional line endings while making the new poem sound unforced, inevitable.

A useful list of types of line breaks from the least to the most disruptive, is provided by Don Paterson as part of his detailed, informative discussion of the line in *The Poem: Lyric, Sign, Metre*. If you are using 'a' or 'the' at the end of the line this will qualify as more disruptive than, for example, enjambment across a clause boundary, and can be a point of discussion. George Szirtes, in his dreamlike, acute meditation on time and language, takes Brooks' line, "We are things of dry hours and the involuntary plan": and strategically italicises, and focusses on, both 'and' and 'the' (along with 'here'):

> This is the *here* and the *and*
> that link our sentences, and this is the one *the*
> we use just the once, our saying involuntary
> as if it could be other, a purpose or a plan.

Another accomplished and natural-sounding golden shovel is Fiona Sampson's 'Travel Literature'. The original line, again taken from Brooks, is: "Whose washed echoes are tremulous down lost halls". Here's Sampson's first stanza:

> All night the trains thunder. Whose
> stories are those, racing away, washed
> clean by the dark? Their echoes
> disturb, disturb, disturb… Stories are what we are –

The two-stanza poem with the echoing of stories to the rhythm of the train and the culmination of the journeys in distant arrival halls, perfectly incorporates and develops Brooks' line. The emphasis on "Whose" at both the beginning of the sentence and the end of the first line points up, at this early stage, the human predicament at the heart of the poem and creates a necessary tension. A surprise the lines accommodate is that the reader doesn't immediately know that 'Whose' is the introducing of a question. In Sampson's last line Brooks' original 'halls' becomes 'arrival halls', encapsulating the idea that the end of a journey is a beginning. In both Sampson's and Szirtes's examples of the form, Brooks' original poem satisfyingly haunts the new poem.

While it's difficult to think of the technical aspects of poetry as separate from each other, it's always as well, of course, to be aware of the possibilities inherent in each feature as part of a contribution to the whole. A skilfully-placed line ending can have something of the feel of the poet having scored a goal, an essential step on the way to the winning of the match.

Further reading:

Pedagogical Sketchbook – Paul Klee, translated by Sibyl Moholy-Nagy (Faber & Faber, 1968).

The Art of the Poetic Line – James Longenbach (Graywolf Press, 2008).

The Collected Poems and Drawings – Stevie Smith (Faber & Faber, 2015).

Brunizem – Sujata Bhatt (Carcanet, 1988).

'The Moses of Michelangelo' (1914) in *Totem and Taboo and Other Works Volume XIII, The Complete Psychological Works of Sigmund Freud* – Sigmund Freud (Vintage, 2001).

Blackbird, Bye Bye – Moniza Alvi (Bloodaxe, 2018).

The Golden Shovel Anthology: New Poems Honoring Gwendolyn Brooks – edited by Peter Kahn, Ravi Shankar and Patricia Smith (The University of Arkansas Press, 2017).

The Poem: Lyric, Sign, Metre – Don Paterson (Faber & Faber, 2018).

Writing Phone Calls:
On Sound in Poetry

Antosh Wojcik

I want to talk to you about poems of sound intention. Ideally, I would be speaking this directly to you, above a neatly curated soundscape that underpins and transposes what I mean in text into sound at the same time – but I'm here, communicating with the raw word, soundless.

Sound intention has a few meanings for me. It means making a poem that is soundly intent; it means making a poem with the intentions of sound. It means thinking about how sound interacts with text and how text interacts with sound.

I hear you. Sound is a vast, abstract thing. Everything is vibrating right now. You've emitted and absorbed sounds in your sleep and you will walk through the day barraged and lulled by sounds. What is noise and more importantly, what is useful noise for our poems?

A poem is a sound structure. A poem can be measured in sound, in metre, rhythm. The tools of assonance, consonance, sibilance (I know, that's a lot of 'ance' sounds) can compose the poem's music. Repetition can give poems a sense of tune and recurrence.

Sound also creates image or can further shape an image in the mind of a listener/reader. When partnered with a poem, the sound is contextualised by the poem's text, and in return, textures the poem.

Working towards sound demands that you, the poet, push how it is that you listen. You must listen to what is around, then what is inside your poem, then how the combination of the two will shape the listening of your work for the reader.

Sound is the freest medium. It's simple and immediate to determine what is inherent in a sound – what that can lead you to think of and what that meaning is, its significance to you.

A poem can read like a confusing sound that someone made and then committed to paper, and we almost struggle with all the things we may be missing or got wrong about its meaning (if there even is a meaning...).

I hear you. 'I can't make sound, I'm no musician, I don't have sound editing software!' No need. We're thinking in sound, like sound, in order to find new possibilities to create and shape our work, even if that means returning our poetry to the silence of a page.

Frank O'Hara wrote about how you could try writing a poem that felt as raw and immediate as a phone call. What happens if we allow our poems to *be* a phone call?

What happens if we take the laws and tools of sound making and apply them to the rules of our poetry? Can text be beyond text on a page – become a physical sound? It's my hope that here we can reach some interesting ways of editing our work and deepen our execution of sound within a work – being definite with why we make a sound, as well as how we did it. Determining what is useful noise.

Sometimes I learn more about writing a poem by watching someone deconstruct their fluency in a certain sound craft.

Watch archive footage of Eric Dolphy playing bass clarinet as part of the Charles Mingus Sextet, 'Take The A Train', Norway, April 12, 1964. His solo takes place from 4'29 until 9'13. The solo is a solo that directs a listener to hear how he breathes in order to create notes. We witness Dolphy reach from the depth of the bass clarinet to propel the instrument to its highest notes in step and mis-step-like phrasings. The band are silent for a duration of the solo and you can hear the very cluck of the clarinet valves as he releases and tunes his breath. We're witnessing how an instrument's structure makes a tune and more so, how Dolphy chooses to hone how we can hear him breathe a note into a sound. It's a breath solo through an instrument.

If the poem is an instrument, we must know how sound plays within it and around it. If we pre-empt the emotion of the text with music or sound, this can neuter the text's power as well as the music. Think what a poem's sound palette is. What is its structure and how is that textured by including sound?

A poet turns to sound because sound is an invisible and intricate force that is essential to the word.

I play drums beneath my poetry. I must decide what the interaction of the word and the strike of the drum is going to be. To accent an already accented aspect of a word means there's a conflict of noise, which is purposeful... or it's not. To drum against what I'm saying? The drums do their thing, I have to not pre-empt the emotion and running of the lines. I can slop the playing to make the words sharper – or I can slop the delivery of the word and sharpen the playing – if it's all slop, what's lost? Most of it. That might be the point? Drumming is a language, a type of speech and is a text. So, the reading of a poem whilst drumming underneath is a duel of languages, speech and text. There is then a balancing required. Are the drums illustrative of the word or is the word illustrative of the drums? Maybe the question doesn't need to be answered, it's that exploration that exacts a truth in both sound and poetry.

Sometimes, sound is a way of making a poem breathe in a new way. It's a means of forging a new listening to your work. It is a sanctuary. The world is a crop of sounds after all. Voices have qualities that environments do. Poems can be pure residues of sounds recorded. It's in the stitching.

Sound is a way of immediately transporting a place to someone. A place doesn't even need to have clear identifiers – a room has ambience and a recorded voice adopts the qualities of the room. Certain rooms shift as the door closes – our last lines in poems are attempts at finding the right door to seal the poem, even if that closing is a flinging wide.

Amy Key's *Poets in Bed* podcast[7] is the perfect example of a simple manipulation, yet hugely effective approach to poem and sound. A poet records themselves reading their work in their bed. Their voice and the reading's ambience take on the sound of the room and the bed. This characterises the reading and causes an immediate intimacy, an immediate listening for us, which ultimately changes how the work reads aloud – even if it's the slightest shift through sound.

To record sound is to document. To write a poem is a self-documentation process but it quickly shifts into a multitude of other things.

Sound is a place of no boundaries, nor binaries. Sound is raw data ready for manipulation.

Poems can be a place of perceived boundaries, perhaps binaries, and our raw data is our self and our ideas of truth. When I say data, I don't really think of computer data, digits, etc. I think of experience and/or boredom, all the significant and seemingly insignificant things that comprise us – that's the raw data for poems.

In the writing of poems, we can have a preoccupation with truth as we seek to carve the things that haunt us and stir us

7   https://soundcloud.com/alabama-may/poets-in-bed-episode-1

into a poem. With this comes the dilemma of stepping through whatever fears you may have of sharing your work and exposing the shit you think about. It hurts to write what hurts and it hurts more to share what hurt you, to make it a tangible sound and structure.

As we dedicate to the truth and cement our personal raw data in word and text, we can enter a fear of the manipulation of our rawness. This manipulation can incur further hurt to the issue we write about – or in the act of manipulation, we fear we are stepping away from the truth, from our raw data. For many reasons, we believe in maintaining the rawness of truth or the initial truth that began the poem.

If we think in terms of sound, the manipulation of truth is essential from the outset.

If you record the sound of something, you are boxing the passing moment; the word, the noise, a truth. It might seem minute but it's a manipulation of a true moment.

As you recite a shopping list into a voice note, you are manipulating the data of what you need to get to eat and feel good for the evening. Storing that passing thought for a poem as a voice note – you made an idea a sound. It will become a poem, but first it was a sound.

I record my Dad mowing the lawn, the flight path knocking above our heads and my sister screaming at Mum in the house. I have immediately manipulated truth with the act of recording. Those moments, whether they happened at the same time or on separate occasions, can now form a soundscape that forms one instance of truth.

The sound is treated; I edit it into one timeframe and suddenly there is a narrative that was not there previously – or it was, but it was not previously connected. A truth of my family life and my place in the world, achieved solely through manipulation.

In sound, these manipulations can go further. I place a delay filter on my Dad's mowing. Delay will make the sound of the lawnmower pan from left to right around a listener's head, trickle and echo away to then resurface. I can make this happen as slowly or evenly or as glitchy as I want. The sound achieves a stark sensation of movement.

Say the mowing is all encompassing but the flight path above our heads is stark – the soundscape feels as though the plane is mowing the sky.

My sister's screaming is the foreground, she sounds as though she is trapped in the mower and this reveals the truth of my Dad and sister's relationship.

I then read a poem over these sounds. The poem could be entirely unrelated or intrinsically related to the sound. For the listener, the layering of word and sound will appear as one unified truth. The poem contextualises the sound, the sound textures the poem.

The dimensions of the truth shift, multiple narratives can be cast.

Perhaps you as the listener are deciding that the plane overhead is the starkest thing in the mix and my sister's shouting is instead something more like an exclamation. This moves the truth of those individual moments into a totally different realm, the first soundscape being an account of my Dad's and my sister's relationship, the second, something far more atmospheric and belonging to the listener, rather than myself.

All of this to say there is an immediacy and urgency to manipulate when you work with sound. What are the possibilities for our poems if we're more willing to manipulate our own raw data from the outset? Nothing in the sound collage is less true; I'd argue that through the manipulation, it's truer, even.

How could this play out in a poem?

Say you documented three events, all unrelated. You use the writing of the poem as a way of bringing the events together – instantly, you're in manipulation mode and you must create ways of bringing these things together. To my mind, that forces the fear of truth to work to the ends of new creative ideas and you've short tracked the worry of manipulating rawness – to me, this gives way to an essential inventiveness as you write the poem.

When you come to rewrite/edit a poem, place a 'filter' on it. You can create any means of filters as you're not working in the confines of a sound editing software where there are limited effects.

Slap a 'dream' filter on a meditative poem about swimming – what emerges from the water? What new meaning rises in the bubbles? You're thinking immediately in the realm of dream – what texture and quality can this bring to the poem?

Place the poem in the centre and attach two sheets to the right and left side. These are 'channels'. Filter out 'breath' in the poem into the right channel and 'sentiment' into the left – how does this break the poem? And how could it be fixed? Unmake to remake.

Imagine the poem is fed through an amplifier and it's set to 'distortion' – what does that do to the piece fed through. What characteristics does the poem take on?

These are all sound intentions that allow a poet to play with their truth and the possibilities our rawness has for a reader. The poem does not need to remain a raw account; it can be manipulated into something beyond its initial capacity as a truth. Through this process, you have reached a new form of the truth that was considered and rigorously created, crafted.

Can you hear me?

I Should Have Called This Essay Something Better, But in Not Doing So Have Thereby Proved One of My Points: On Titling Your Poems

Rishi Dastidar

There's one thing I really want you to take away from this series of apercus, barbs and attempts at epigrams failing to masquerade as an essay.

I don't want you to ever title one of your poems 'Rain' ever again. Honestly, that's it.

At some level this whole book is a roundabout attempt to smuggle this message out into the poetic community. It's so important to me that I'll repeat it at the end too. I'll explain why I take this seemingly extreme and arbitrary position in a bit, but for now, know that if I can persuade just *one* of you to scratch that option – that thought – from your titling practices, then my work is done.

Why focus on what some people think of as the least important part of the poem?

My contention here is that the title of a poem is the most important part of a poem that we pay the least amount of attention to. Consider: when was the last time you might have seen a review of a poem or a book that also makes mention of whether the title of said poem or book is good or bad, happy or sad, sticking together whatever the weather?

Or alternatively, when was the last time that in a workshop or mentoring session you spent as much time on the title as opposed to your first line, last line, all the other lines in-between, your rhyme scheme, your form, your images? Chances are that a) you didn't, b) you didn't think you had to, assuming that a title would magically appear, delivered by the Poem Titler's branch of FedEx[8], or c) you didn't think it mattered all that much because, hey! it's only a title after all. Consider what follows as a ham-fisted attempt to at least ridicule that last belief into permanent abeyance.

You are obsessed by titles, aren't you? Absurdly so in fact.

That I have been collecting potential titles for my second, now, third collection is a matter of record, and a semi-public Google Doc is available on request. Is it an obsession? Yes, but then a) what is a writer without an obsession or five? b) it could be worse, it could be an obsession about footnotes.[9]

Another reason for this state of affairs is the very real envy I have of those writers who can conceive of, begin, and finish a poem around a topic or subject or incident, and only then cast around for a title to provide a capstone for the work. I look at these people with no little awe: how do they do that? Me, I can't write unless there's a glimmer of a title in sight, or an actual title ready to go, however much I know it might change at a later date. What can I say, I like knowing where I'm starting from when I'm writing. But it also speaks to the very real need that I have to try and frame, encapsulate, pin down the idea I'm trying to communicate from the off – a psychological crutch I now realise, so I don't ever truly get lost when writing, and at least have a sense of where I need to get back to.

---

8   Actually, that's not a bad business idea; can somebody check if
     'titlex.co.uk' is free please?
9   Seriously, this is an insignificant number of footnotes for me;
     delusional rather than obsessional.

Why though? What tragic event in your formative years led us to this hectoring yet obsessional pass?

I would like to credit – note, not blame – my time spent as a sub-editor for various newspapers and magazines. For those of you not *au fait* with the world of journalism, the 'subs' are the people whose task it is to take the raw copy or words that are filed by reporters and writers, then edit and shape them to fit the available space, add polish and sparkle as desired. They will remove errors and potential legal howlers, and probably most importantly of all find a form of words to sit atop the piece that will act as both sales pitch, and pithy summary, to tempt the passing, casual reader to stop flicking through the pages and instead read this story instead of any other right now.

That I am as obsessed by headlines as I am the titles of poems is perhaps no surprise.

But consider: in the same way that I had a responsibility to the original writers of those words, so you too have a responsibility to the rest of the words in your poem, to find the formulation that does the best, most persuasive job of bringing people to it, so they can discover the poem, and read it for themselves.

I mean, I assume that you want people to read your work, right?[10]

This is all sounding horribly like the business of selling. I came to poetry to get away from that.

Which I understand, and heaven knows, even I get tired of my day job of being a handmaiden to capitalism. But it would be remiss of me not to point out that titles of works of culture

---

10   I am aware that some of you at this point might be about to argue that while the above peroration might be true in the context of solo poems of your own floating about in the pages of magazines or the whirl of social media, it might be less so in the case of your own books and pamphlets, as you have, as it were, already sealed the deal with them. And to that I say unto you: pshaw! Book readers are as likely to jump around, grazing and browsing your wares in a non-linear order – so why not, while they are doing that, remind them of your fire-cracker verbal brilliance every time they come back to your contents page?

can help sell said works, or at least help to. As poet Kathryn Simmonds writes in her essay on the subject of titles:

> Thinking back I only picked up *The Unbearable Lightness of Being* for its enigmatic title and though I was a bit disappointed to find it featured a slightly seedy bloke and his sexual conquests, the title had nonetheless worked its magic. Another copy sold.[11,12]

Think of it this way: your title is your poem's shop window – an opportunity to make sure it gets the eyeballs it deserves. And it'd be a shame to miss out by underselling your poem by being coy, modest, bashful. It's an opportunity in other ways too: if your poem is a riddle, can the title provide the clue? If your poem is a punchline, can the title be the set-up? If your poem is a magic trick, can your title be the wand?

But poems didn't used to have titles, so why all the fuss?

Very true, and of course you can adopt that as a strategy now as well. Can I just gently suggest though, that no one will read a poem that appears with the words *Untitled [57]* atop it with anything other than a sense of weary duty. And I sure didn't get into this game for that.

Of course, if you are the reincarnation of Emily Dickinson then you don't actually need titles for your poems. But then you're a genius, and don't actually need any help from me.

Didn't Terrance Hayes use the same title for all his poems in his recent book, *American Sonnet For My Past And Future Assassin*? I don't see you telling him off.

Well a) he's also a genius, b) look at how resonant, dynamic, thrilling, darkly unsettling, political and factually communicative

---

11   https://magmapoetry.com/archive/magma-51/articles/working-titles/
12   Of course, we are in the realm of the subjective here. Kevin Jackson, in his book dedicated to titles and all sorts of invisible forms within literature, says *TULOB*, as I shall never call it again, is both a chunky mouthful and also unforgettable. Kevin Jackson, *Invisible Forms* (Picador, 1999)

his titular phrase is.... and, c) then look how he goes bolder yet still; by giving all of his poems the same title he means to make sure we never lose sight of his target. It's the poetic equivalent of being looked at dead in the eye.

Right, enough of the theory. How does someone begin to reach this state of exalted titular nirvana?

Ah, the dreaded practical part of any advice-giving essay. Let me preface what follows by saying that while I believe in my tips, you are of course at liberty to break my rules. I'm kind like that:

1. Embrace ambiguity: this perhaps is the root of my aversion to 'Rain' as a title, and single word titles generally.[13] It's hard to get that mystery and intrigue – qualities that might draw a reader in – in a single word that doesn't feel overly 'poetic'.
2. What happens when you juxtapose unexpected words and ideas? Does something more memorable emerge? Chances are it does.
3. Don't settle for your first idea: Elizabeth Bishop's 'One Art' was once called something else – it's worth discovering what, then thinking about why she might have changed it.
4. Don't be scared of the long title, that goes on and on, hopefully in a more entertaining way than this clause: and also, note that they don't have to be elaborate set ups demanding a pay off in the poem's last line. They can just be, well, long.
5. Can't settle on one title? Why not have two? You don't see this used as much but an 'or' (I like using 'a/k/a'[14]) not only allows you to do your juxtaposing, but also makes your title longer...

---

13   Yes, I have single word titles in my poems, don't @ me.
14   'Also known as', a form I've stolen from the late David Foster Wallace

6. Stealing from other works is permissible[15], but then the poem really must live up to the theft.

7. Challenge yourself: As literary critic Kevin Jackson says, a title should be a small work of art in its own right. Do yours have the potential to enter wider culture?

Ideally your title should be a frame within which your poem is set; a summary of what might be in it; an invitation to the reader to read it; and a way of selling it to a disinterested world. Even better if it can fulfil all four of those tasks at once.

Oh, and don't forget, if your title is good enough, then you won't need to write the rest of the poem. Something I know appeals to all of us, secretly.[16]

I suppose that you'll now tell me that actually working harder on poem titles is actually a vital artistic and public service too.

Exactly so! There is an old saw that the main role of poets is actually to provide titles for novelists to use on top of their own magnum opi. Don't let them down: who knows what slices of literary, nay global history, might otherwise be different without you? Jackson, in his book *Invisible Forms* notes: "*A Farewell to Arms* just happens to be one example of a title which Hemingway settled on and stuck to unswervingly, but it certainly didn't come to him in a blinding flash – he set himself to trawling through Sir Arthur Quiller-Couch's *Oxford Book of English Verse* in search of inspiration when he had already completed a 600-page manuscript of a novel."[17]

---

15   I would feel ooky borrowing a phrase from another poem, but have no such qualms for liberating something from a novel, a song lyric or a film title. The Nine Arches legal eagles at this point would also like it made clear that: whilst it is permissible they strongly advise that you credit where it is due in your notes or acknowledgements, so as to avoid any misunderstanding that could construe it as plagiarism, especially if you are borrowing from another literary, or less well-known, work.

16   The most famous – and most pleasing – example of this particular showing off is, of course, Don Paterson's 'On Going to Meet a Zen Master in the Kyushu Mountains and Not Finding Him'.

17   Jackson, *ibid.*

Go on then, make your case as to why you are so against 'Rain' as a title for a poem...

It's not that I hate the word 'rain' per se (I do hate rain, but that's another essay entirely), but that it has been done, used by a poem that I'm pretty sure you're all familiar with already. That being so, why are you ignoring Pound's dictum about making things new when it comes to your title? Do you think there was a footnote that said, yeah but not for the thing topping your poems? It *all* needs to be made new, not nearly all of it.

There is only one exception to this: if you happen to have written the best poem ever about rain. If you're sure you have, then go for it. But even then, I'd still change it if I were you.

Wasn't actually joking about repeating the beginning of the essay; here is the one thing you really need to take away from this essay.

Do not call one of your poems 'Rain'. I'll find out. I'll know, even if you just have it as a working title that you tell yourself you'll change before submitting it somewhere.

And no, you can't use 'Precipitation' instead.

Notes From the Notebook:
On the Writing of 'Nine Nights'

Malika Booker

1.

When I first started writing poetry I was addicted to the act of learning my craft. I felt that poetry was a vocation, not unlike being a carpenter where the difference between being talented and producing excellent work depends on dedication and training. At about the same time Spread the Word, a literature development organisation, opened in South London, just a five minute walk from my home in Brixton; I spent the next three years enrolled on as many of their short story, novel writing and poetry courses as I could manage. For over 15 or more years, my evenings and weekends were devoted to attending poetry workshops and residentials run by them, the Poetry School, Arvon and many others, as well as going to various literature festivals. This addiction only stopped after I graduated from Goldsmiths, University of London in 2014 with an MA in Creative and Life Writing.

Not only did I religiously complete the assignments from these workshops, but I bought poetry craft books like: *The Art and Craft of Poetry* by Michael J Bujega; *Writing Poetry* by WN Herbert; *The Making of a Poem: A Norton Anthology of Poetic Forms* by Eavan Boland and Mark Strand; and *On Poetry* by Glyn Maxwell[18]. I would sit at my writing desk devouring these craft essays and trying every single exercise in the books no matter how difficult. These exercises yielded strong drafts and poems, but more often than not a higher proportion ended

---

18   Michael J Bujega, *The Art and Craft of Poetry* (Publishers Digest, 1994); WN Herbert, *Writing Poetry* (Routledge, 2009); Eavan Boland and Mark Strand, *The Making of a Poem: A Norton Anthology of Poetic Forms* (WW Norton, 2001), Glyn Maxwell, On Poetry (Oberon Books, 2017)

up being discarded, remaining in a notebook that will never see the light of day. In hindsight, I now realise that craft is really the building of your writing muscles. Having an arsenal of formal knowledge, practices and strategies to draw upon during the process of poem making, in order to facilitate your movement from an idea to the completed draft. So, in order to understand how a poem was made, one must scrutinise the writing process as it unfolded in the notebook.

2.

This essay aims to go behind the scenes and extract text from the making of my poem 'Nine Nights', a long sequence published in *The Poetry Review*'s Autumn 2016 issue, and shortlisted for the Forward Prize for best single poem in 2017.

Nine Nights is a funerary tradition practised in the Caribbean. The wake usually begins on the evening after the deceased has died, where family and friends visit the house to share memories, sing hymns, drink and eat as well as play dominos and cards. In the Bible, in the Book of John, Jesus brings Lazarus of Bethany back to life four days after he died. As I listened to my mother's stories from the funerals that she attended I began to wonder what would happen if Lazarus was Grenadian, resurrected and walked back into his own Nine Nights wake?

My last collection *Pepper Seed* was autobiographical so I wanted to move away from writing personal narratives. As a black Caribbean poet I wanted to re-imagine and re-locate my family's experiences, language, church, religion, ritual, and faith into a biblical poetic by inserting the Caribbean landscape into a biblical one.

3.

I am going to take you through five different phases of progress I made in the notebook as I wrote the poem.

First: the initial act of writing. Here it is a willful act of beginning, a brave moment of jumping into the white space, the unknown. I am starting to commit to the poem, as well as gather and allow core elements from my subconscious to surface. The following words were the first scribbles that I made in my notebook:

Lazarus   village in Grenada   Sister Mary
anointed
the Lord with
ointment
wiped feet with
her hair
Lain in the grave 4 days (John 11:17)
"thy brother shall rise again" (John 11:23)
keep things – resurrect and the life
take away the stone (John 11:39)

Here I seem to be a poet casting a net but struggling to catch any fish. I am also instinctively noting down quotes from the biblical text, as well as foraging around for root words. 'Resurrect' is circled and underlined, as if even at this early stage I suspect that this will become one of the major thematic elements of the poem.

Key words: Nine nights , wake, family
gathered together, feast and supper

Quotes: Lord by this time he stinketh: for
He hath been dead four days John (11:39)

'Stinketh' is also underlined and circled several times in my notebook as if I sense another important sensory element – a key to the poem. I begin to explore the relevance of this scent by writing:

Fart – try to find your way into this stench – What does
the stench of Death smell like? Will it stick to Lazarus if he
returns to his wake on the fourth day?

4.

Second: research and poetic conversation. After pages of circling and exploring to discover, I begin to write notes to myself:

> Please read, read, read the gospel according to John over and over now. Try to get beneath the story.

So I immerse myself in the gospel, and fill the pages in my notebook with quotes, anecdotes and commentary of John's Gospel. I seem to be interrogating this biblical narrative, and its main characters, in an effort to understand the core. Whilst reading the Bible I also seem to be rooting around trying to find my own hook. Then I hit a wall.

Whenever my writing and ideas stall, pushing me into a scary space where I feel that I don't know what I'm doing, I revisit Yehuda Amichai's selected poems, set the timer on my mobile phone for 50 minutes and read, stopping occasionally to copy one line quotes from a poem or transcribe the entire poem into my notebook. It is as if this necessary act of conversing with other collections enables my poetic imagination to leap, make discoveries, or even have a brief respite.

At that time I also happened to be reading Kei Miller's collection, *The Cartographer Tries to Map a Way to Zion*. Miller's work caused me to listen to Bunny Wailer's song 'The Blackheart Man' on repeat. Somehow the combined stimulus of Amichai, Miller and Wailer enabled me to begin constructing a narrative as well as build the character of Lazarus, imagining him as a tall dark blue-black handsome Rasta man. I began to question how this Rasta man would react once he found himself raised from the dead?

> – he danced skank and bounced
> – fingers clicking as rude bwoy
> – dance for joy – bruk out of
> – his body, that body that had

112

    – been dead, prone, and marble, a heavy thing
    – there was a reggae song, a scat, a bun down Babylon,
    and hymns,
    – a guitar and Bunny Wailer's Black Heart Man lick down
    from mouths,
    – parched of hymns

Conversations with other writers, poets and historical texts is a vital part of my crafting process and can yield surprising results, enabling significant leaps and discoveries. The readings enabled me to begin to construct scenes, settings, tones, and begin to suggest possibilities for the voice and musicality of the poem.

5.

Third: grounding, staying focussed. At this point I would begin setting underlying goals and intentions, asking myself what I want to achieve in the poem, reminding myself of what I want to do. These could take the form of affirmations that led to a burst of text that illustrated or began to form my aims and intentions of the poem. For instance, after writing:

    – I aim to capture a sense of wonder
    – Aim to write humour
    – Aim to write a joyful poem

I began to construct the following – maybe a scene of the reaction of the mourners at the wake to Lazarus's resurrection:

    Who pass out and had to get sap with
    Limacol and soft candle
    How Miss Gibbs forget her hips
    bad till she run two steps
    and fall brat taps
    Uncle Johnny flinging rum on the
    floor boards shouting go back, go back
    How the wake bruk up when Lazarus get fast up, in he skin
    and decide to jump out of death's skin.

6.

Four: conversation with self. My notes now attempt to establish what the poem seeks to achieve, and any more research tasks needed. It is commonplace at Caribbean funerals for one of the mourners to share their dreams where the symbols foretold the death.

I am beginning to construct the building blocks of the poem. A set of bricks that hint at the possible construction; but I am also concerned with grounding my work and staying focused:

- Remember you are writing toward a biblical poetic or writing a biblical poem.
- Note to self: Look up symbolism for dreams that mean death.
- maybe there are dreams – that cannot be explained – flying fish.
- fish in flight – no one can interpret. How fish flying over water with humming birds.
- Eddo swelling under the bed of earth, pushes the soil up.
- Remember to combine the reality of the everyday with an underlying sense of rhythm and myth.

7.

Fifth: Structure begins to assert itself. The Nine Nights wake begins to impose a structure. The poem will be a sequence, with nine sections, verse paragraphs of nine lines. Line breaks could be between five and ten syllables:

Day 1: 1st Night – The Set Up
1.   Corn soup bubbled in the stove
2.   Red beans slowly merged with rice
3.   In coconut milk – chairs
4.   Gathered in clusters. Dominos and
5.   Rum were set up on the table
6.   Glasses wiped. That first evening

7. The mourners arrived shuffling
8. Under the shock of it all,
9. Suddenness, the priest opened the
10. Gathering with prayer and a mother fell down under the weight of her dead son. "So young" she muttered "so young"

As I begin to give shape to the words I write with a calypso mix playing quietly in the background, as a way of evoking rhythm and a sense of place. I seem to also allow the last line to break the form as if I aware that the narrative thread is more important than the shape at this moment:

7th Night – fling down party
1. that moon light him dance to
2. Blackheart man by Bunny Wailer
3. What ah way him bruk out. The
4. rude bwoy skank, dash
5. way hymns from the house – cleanse
6. it out with the heavy ; black
7. speaker box vibrating. *Give*
8. *thanks*, it trembled, as his foot
9. rise up and skip, as his fingers lick together and the rasta man skank tek over when Lazarus start dance fire and brimstone, start chant, chant down Babylon and lick wall, shouting *more fire*, the joy of alive putting springs in his step. He locs swinging like twine tied to breath – yelling over and over *I & I levity.*

Here is the joy I wanted the poem to embrace, Lazarus partying from the sheer joy of being alive.

I began to imagine that the next step this handsome Rasta would make would be to bedazzle a woman with chat-up lyrics shaped by a surreal language, as if he is a professor of resurrection:

8th Night – Geography of resurrection.

1. when the reporter ask him what it
2. was like in that dim room with the
3. pale cream walls & the hum of mosquito
4. he say, there is a geography to
5. being resurrected. A map that have
6. swamp and crossroads, that have
7. sweet water stairs and thorny
8. paths. There is a one foot in front of
9. another map. A believe and it shall be map. A
   surrender map and you just have to trod it all
   rude gal, you just have to trod it.

8.

Sixth: Editing – moving from the notebook to the computer. The construction of the poem takes place there, where I can consider shape, cut and paste. The poem forms itself into prose blocks, reminiscent of the layout of the text in the Bible.

Nine Nights – The Wake

1st Night: The Set up

If you did see people that first night. People for so. Who come from town, from far like St David, from near like St Marks to this little St John parish. It had the makings of a good funeral. Pure bus park up by Gouyave roadside like ants. Them mourners arrived, shuffling with the shock. The priest opened up that wake with plenty prayers. Corn soup bubbled in the iron pot, red beans slowly converged with rice, thyme and coconut milk. Chairs clustered together like fowls in the yard. Till he mother fell down under the weight of her dead son. *So young* she muttered, *so young.*

9.

I hope that this demonstrated that whilst I have a theoretical notion of craft and process, the reality is messy and in the moment – and the only way to understand the methodology of the crafting of a particular poem is to revisit the notebook. An illuminating exercise, that enabled me to understand that there is no single method or rules for writing a poem. Instead, each is a single individual, with personalised demands and needs.

PART THREE

ON BRINGING POEMS TO LIFE

Digging Up The Word Hoard: On Using All of Your Voice in Poetry

Liz Berry

When I first began writing poems using Black Country dialect it was like digging up my own Staffordshire Hoard. The area where I'd grown up, too often mocked for its accent and dialect, turned out to be a field full of spectacular words, sounds and phrases. Everywhere I looked, the stuff of poetry was glinting out of the muck. *Tranklements, donkey-bite, jack-squalor...* It was utterly irresistible. I wondered how its richness had remained hidden from the wider world of literature for so long.

Yet the more I read, the more I realised that Black Country dialect wasn't alone. Although I'd discovered and loved beautiful poetry in other voices, Scots in particular, there were countless lyrical, thrilling, gutsy vernaculars[19] alive within our country which were almost entirely absent from contemporary British lyric poetry – poetry which sings of love, families, place, loss. I wanted readers and listeners like me, and not at all like me, to be able to find the languages of their mums and sisters, boyfriends and sons, in poetry, and to feel that those voices were recognised and celebrated. Who was to say what was and wasn't the language of poetry? I felt furious and inspired.

Before I could begin writing the poems, I needed to tune my ears to the right frequency. If you want to write in any kind of vernacular then you have to be able to hear it in your head first; it's a living thing that you're trying to capture on the page, and so it has to begin in your mind and mouth. Choose language which feels close to your heart, from your own

---

19   Vernacular is simply living speech, the everyday language that's used by people in a particular region, social/cultural group or speech community.

speech community. Don't fret that you don't have an accent or a dialect interesting enough for poetry; remember each of our individual voices contains within it multiple versions – the voice we use with our partners, with our children, with our hometown friends, taxi drivers, the voice we'd use to give a speech, sing or take tea with the Queen. These are all versions of our voice: nuanced, complex, ever shifting and entirely unique. Bringing a feel of the vernacular to your poems can be as simple as allowing yourself to use the full range of your voice – slang, home words[20], invented words, varying patterns of phrasing and grammar – all these things can conjure a sound and a poetry which feels beguilingly alive. So many of us feel we have to tidy up our voices in order to be taken seriously as poets, that our voices might not belong in poetry, so think of this as a permission-giving, a rebellion.

Before I picked up my pencil, I spent hours listening to Black Country and Brummie dialects being spoken by friends, relatives, old men in the pubs with their wammels and pints of Banks' Bitter, my friends' kids, teenage girls on the bus. I read the gospels in Black Country dialect – "God ud promised we wen Adam an Eve fust sinned thar a saivyer ud cum"[21] – made my family groan with the *Black Country Joke Book* and was inspired by the lads whose local printing business had revived 'The Black Country Alphabet' – *K is for Kaylied, T is for Tara-A-Bit…* The language was thrilling: sometimes tough and muscular like *clem-gutted* (thin and miserable looking) or *ommered* (hammered), other times soft and delicate as *jeth* (death) and *mither* (bother or annoy). By listening you get a feel for what each word might bring to a poem – creating a voice, giving a sense of place, expressing defiance or tenderness.

---

20   'Home words' are those delightful strange words invented within families or close knit groups, often in childhood, which linger on. Home words might also mean words from a home language and for those interested in exploring bilingual poetry I'd direct them to the wonderful Harana Poetry journal: www.haranapoetry.com

21   Fletcher, Kate. *The Gospels in Black Country Dialect.* (Black Country Society, 1989)

Listening makes you attentive and respectful too, something that's crucial when working with vernaculars. Too frequently vernacular speech has been employed crudely, to suggest someone uneducated or foolish, but turn that around and see what happens when you lift the vernacular up and use it to celebrate, explore, play, to show eloquence and poetry in the voices that inspired you.

Tracking down the vernacular

I found guidance and inspiration from other poets who used vernacular language. There's a rich and rebellious history of vernacular writing, of poets and novelists reclaiming the language of their communities as the language of literature. I devoured the wonderful *Faber Book of Vernacular Verse*, edited by Tom Paulin[22], (its introduction alone is magical) and read contemporary vernacular poetry from writers as varied as Kathleen Jamie, Daljit Nagra, Malika Booker, Kei Miller and Katrina Porteous. I read novels in vernacular – *Huckleberry Finn*, *God's Own Country* by Ross Raisin – and listened to music from groups like the wonderful Unthanks who use the vernacular of the North East in their songs. When vernacular writing works it makes everything seem zingy and alive, what Paulin lovingly describes in his introduction as "the springy irreverent, chanting, quartzy, often tender and intimate, vernacular voice... a language impatient of print, an orality which seeks to fly through its authoritarian net". Although much of the language was old, indeed writing using dialect can be an act of preservation, it felt fresh and different, subversive somehow.

Vernacular writing is also an inherently political act and is often used to challenge ideas of standardisation and authority. A beautiful example of this is Kei Miller's collection *The Cartographer Tries To Map A Way To Zion*, in which the vibrant vernacular voice of the Rastaman is set against the flat standard English of the Cartographer. Or as the little sow in

---

22   *The Faber Book of Vernacular Verse.* ed. Tom Paulin. (Faber, 1990)

my vernacular poem 'Sow' sticks up her trotters to the cockerel on the spire, her language also sticks up its trotters to standard English and the ways it represents and misrepresents the bodies and voices of working class women.

I also made it my mission to know as much as possible about Black Country dialect and this is helpful no matter what vernacular you're working with. Track down any poems, books, songs or dictionaries containing your vernacular and immerse yourself in the language. Local libraries, museums, small presses and local history societies are useful sources. Spend time writing down some of your favourite words and exploring their meaning. Discover any other poets or writers who've written using your dialect and read their work – good, bad and ugly. Even if the poems aren't your cup of tea then you might pick up some interesting words or ways of recording phonetically. You'll understand what's gone before you and what new perspective or approach you might be able to bring.

Eventually I started tentatively writing poems which included a few dialect words, testing the boundaries, before attempting to write in my own version of Black Country. I use the word 'version' because the exciting and liberating thing about vernacular writing is its fluidity. Oral language is impossible to pin down definitively – it's a shape-shifting and constantly evolving creature; and so I aimed to write in a way that sought to capture its spirit, to engage with that playfulness and willingness to make-new. I enjoyed mixing dialect and standard words together, experimenting with sound and meaning. I wove old, almost forgotten words in with new and invented words, wanting to carry them forward for a new generation of readers and speakers. Above all, I wanted the voices in the poems to feel alive and urgent and to let the thrill of the language lead me into new and unexpected places. When writing using the vernacular, it is important to keep it fresh. Even if the language you're drawing on is from an earlier time, keep the rest of the poem – form, phrasing, ideas – contemporary. To see this in action, read or listen to Jay Bernard's devastating poems in *Surge* or Harry Josephine Giles' zingy rebellious 'magpie' Scots in *Tonguit*.

Homes, open to all

For me there were then important choices to be made. How could the poems capture the vernacular in a way that felt convincing and recognisable to local readers without shutting out those from other regions? How to create poems which felt alive and not museum pieces? I wanted the poems to be open to all. The best poets are able to write about places that are very particular to them but do so in a way that opens them up to others, or makes readers think about their own homes and voices. Many of us know what it's like to leave a place behind, or to be homesick, to love someone from somewhere, to long to go back and be the person you were.

Although this might seem slippery in a book about poetic craft, the technical details, the nitty gritty, are something each writer has to decide on for themselves. Knowing vernacular poetry is both personal and deeply political, each writer must make choices based upon their intentions. How much will you help your readers or require of them? I chose to give a small glossary at the foot of each page in my book to make it easy for readers to understand and enjoy the unfamiliar words without being held up. Other poets like Nagra and Jen Hadfield include a single glossary at the end of their books; some don't gloss at all but instead place the onus upon the reader to discover the words for themselves or to be, for once, the ones excluded by language.

The question of phonetic spelling is a trickier one. Phonetic spelling can guide a reader to the correct pronunciation and give them a flavour of the spoken word but, on the flipside, it can be unreliable, difficult to read or too distracting. For me it was a process of trial and error, finding a balance somewhere between the two: a few of my poems have elements of phonetic spelling mixed in with the standard, whilst other poems are written entirely in the standard with only a word or two of dialect. It's experimentation: constantly rewriting rules and being prepared to make mistakes. It's also about learning when to hold back. You don't need to throw everything at every poem. Sometimes the odd word or grammatical variation is all it takes to lift the work. Think of that perfect old Scots word *beglamoured* in Robin Robertson's 'At Roane Head' or Roy McFarlane's final wounding line in 'Clinton McCurbin, 1987', a poem about police brutality, the only line in the poem in vernacular: *"babylon a kill we off and nobody nuh see"*.

Smuggling words across the border

Indeed if you're drawn to vernacular writing and curious about trying it then this tentative, subtle approach is a good place to start. The poet Paul Batchelor once spoke of it as "smuggling words across the border", an analogy I like as it suggests something of the rebellious, subversive power of the vernacular. Another playful route in is to make a vernacular translation of one of your own short poems or a poem by another poet. These little exercises might never see the world outside your notebook, but they're good practice for getting a feel of the voice and what effects it might bring. Be patient with yourself during these experiments; you're trying something new, opening up a voice that might have been closed off for a while, so don't be disappointed if the magic isn't instant. I've got countless folders of 'not quite' poems which I like to think of as the compost from which the green shoots of real poems might grow.

If this still feels daunting, then go out into the world and listen to vernacular poetry being spoken and sung. Go to readings and track down recordings and videos of poets performing their work. You'll be bowled over by how alive it feels, how electric, and you'll return in-love and inspired. I've been across the country and beyond, reading poems in the vernacular of my small, little-known-about region and the response has been extraordinary and deeply moving. What's apparent is that vernacular writing still generates great emotional response in readers. It's a challenging and surprising way of writing, even in today's Britain, alive with multiple voices and vernaculars. Readers long for voices which feel vivid and real to them, to be transported by poetry, shown other worlds.

And I believe this is why vernacular writing continues to enchant, to move us in ways that standard English alone cannot. Just as we marveled at the treasures dug up from a rainy Staffordshire field, thrilled to discover news of life from a hidden world, so we take pleasure in the rich hoards of language held within communities. When poets use vernaculars, they lift this language to the light, show us its force and its beauty, reveal what it has to tell us about old and new, belonging and leaving, wum and away.

Write What You Know and Then Write Something Even Better: On Creating Characters and Personas in Poems

Dean Atta

No matter how much imagination or metaphor you employ, no matter whether you change the gender, age, ethnicity or even the species of your speaker, people will still assume your poems are about you. And they always are. You choose to write about something or someone because you have a point you want to get across or a fascination you want to explore.

We are told to write what we know but you do not have to inhabit another's body to know them. We can know someone through our relationship with, exposure to, and observations of them. We can also imagine inhabiting their body and living through an experience as them. Our imagination is informed by conversations, reading, listening, viewing, as well as our own lived experience. We can invent people, who may be an approximation of ourselves or someone else in the real world but who is free to explore imaginary scenarios without real world consequences.

This is exactly what I did when writing my verse novel *The Black Flamingo*. I wanted to use some of my real life experiences in the story but I didn't want to be tied down by the facts or timeline of my own life. Thus, the character of Michael was born. Michael has the same mixed race heritage, sexual orientation and many of the same interests as me, but most importantly he is not me. I could write and re-write many versions of Michael's first kiss and sexual experience, fights with his best friend, coming out as gay to his mother, standing up to school bullies, until I got it right, until the poems said what I wanted them to say or what I realised they needed to say.

When I shared an extract of the book with a group of young people on an Arvon retreat I was tutoring, one boy put up his hand and asked, "Is it about a bird or a boy?" I answered, "Both." But the flamingo is a metaphor. I had researched flamingo mating, parenting, and fighting to find ways to say the things I didn't have human language for. Because I was writing about a boy who felt different to other boys, different to his family, who didn't quite know who he was. I wanted to find a way for my readers to feel this too, so maybe Michael has feathers?

Reflecting on the experience of writing Michael's story in *The Black Flamingo*, I come to realise that all of my other poems, which I present as being about me, Dean Atta, are also an approximation, a character, a persona, a fiction of sorts. This may be for several reasons. It could be that I change details to protect myself or another person. It could be that I want to defamiliarise or distance myself from a traumatic event. It could be because the facts don't make the best poem. Because it would be more convenient if their eyes were green and not blue or we meet them in a library and not a nightclub. You reach an impasse where there is the poem of fact and the poem of possibility. But if you change every detail, are you still writing about something that you actually know? And when should that matter? Why should the facts stand in the way of you writing the best poem you are capable of? We know about so-called poetic licence but often feel beholden to the facts of our own life.

Spaces for empathy

Perhaps you don't want to write as yourself, or even a version of yourself? Perhaps you want to write as someone completely different? Look up Patricia Smith's poem 'Skinhead'. Even if you have read or watched it before, read and watch it again. For those unable to do so right now, let me tell you about it. This persona poem by Smith is in the voice of a racist and homophobic white America man. Giving voice to this white male speaker, Smith, an African-American woman, calls black people "niggers" and gay men "fags". We as the reader or audience know not to hear them as Smith's words even though they are in her poem. The poem is violent and confrontational but also greatly empathetic to its speaker. Smith wears his white skin so well that you see both the white male speaker and black female poet in every word choice.

I believe it matters that 'Skinhead' was written and performed by an African-American woman and not a white person or even a mixed race gay man such as myself. If 'Skinhead' were a monologue from a play or an extract from a novel we might simply see the skinhead character but as a poem it is about Smith trying on his white skin and trying out his self-righteous voice. Voicing his abhorrent views, whilst allowing him a backstory and human frailty is a lesson in empathy. Why should we care what a racist homophobe thinks and feels? Is it because their thoughts and feelings might turn into actions that cause us pain and suffering? Or simply because they, too, are suffering and that is worth our attention and understanding?

You may feel like you don't have time to empathise with racists and homophobes, and I wouldn't blame you, but the poetry that matters most to me is strongly about empathy. Claudia Rankine's lyric essay *Citizen* makes space for empathy over and over again as it catalogues a series of micro-aggressions, small and insidious acts of racism that many black people face every single day. Malika Booker's *Pepper Seed* makes space for empathy for black women who have been hurt by colonialism, sexism, and each other. Raymond Antrobus' *The Perseverance* most notably makes space for empathy for D/deaf people.

Andrew McMillan's *physical* and *playtime* make space for empathy for men suffering due to toxic masculinity. The poetry of Ocean Vuong and Warsan Shire make space for empathy for refugees. The poetry and flash fiction of Travis Alabanza and Gray Crosbie make space for empathy for transgender people. All of the aforementioned poets' works do so much more than that, they explore love, loss, longing and belonging, and speak with many voices.

When I think of character writing my mind soon drifts beyond poetry to songs, such as "Four Women" by Nina Simone. In this song, four female characters speak in sequence to show that the experience of the African-American woman is not singular. These women are archetypes rather than stereotypes, and we, the listener, understand that these four are but four of many. Although Simone was also an African-American woman, we wouldn't say any of these four are her own voice or lived experience. Simone seems to have found authentic and everlasting voices for Aunt Sarah, Safronia, Sweet Thing and Peaches.

If you, poet, want to speak outside of your own lived experience, you are allowed to do so. But be aware of two things. One: Why do you want to do it? Two: How will you pull it off?

First, the why.

Do you want to better understand and empathise with someone who has wronged you? Do you want to write a bridge between your experience and theirs? Do you want to highlight some universal truth that transcends race, gender, sexuality, age, etc? Or are you simply just bored of writing about yourself?

It's worth keeping in mind that so much of our lived experience is informed by our race, gender, sexuality, age, etc. My experience is as a mixed-race gay man. I am non-disabled and do not have a long-term physical health condition. One might say that being disabled is not part of my experience but I would flip it and say being non-disabled is a big part of my experience because I experience privileges that some disabled people will not, due to lack of access. If I were to write about being blind or deaf or in a wheelchair or having chronic pain, my reason would be twofold; to challenge non-disabled readers to think about what they take for granted and recognise their privilege and then to think about how they can share or give up some of this privilege and provide better access for disabled people.

Immerse yourself

Now, the how.

If you're a man and you want to write in the voice of a woman you know well, such as your mother or sister, friend or partner, you might use things they have said to you and observations you have made through your relationship with them. But if you want to write in the voice of a woman you have never met in a country you have never been to, you may struggle to pull this off with any authenticity or nuance.

If you are cisgender (not transgender) and you think simply using they/them pronouns (instead of he/him or she/her) makes the subject of your poem non-binary (neither male or female), you are being disingenuous and failing to understand the complexity of being non-binary in a violently-gendered society. Words like "he" and "she", "ladies" and "gentlemen", "sir" and "madam" are just one of the easily comprehensible ways of misgendering someone. Non-binary people may also receive multiple micro- and macro-aggressions, such as looks of confusion and disgust, ignorant and offensive questions and comments, threats and physical attack, ongoing bullying in their home, school, university or workplace, lack of gender-neutral toilets, and inadequate healthcare provision. So, if as a cisgender poet you are writing from a cisgender perspective and then changing the pronouns to they/them, this probably won't read as authentic to non-binary people or those who know them well.

If you want any character or persona in your poetry to feel authentic, you have to do your research. You must read, listen and watch everything you can about people like them, poetry, fiction, non-fiction, songs, movies, documentaries – immerse yourself – and, where it is possible to do so, spend time with people like them. Make sure you have way more backstory for them than you would ever need to show in your writing, because ultimately it will show in how caricature or nuanced they feel to those who have had similar experiences. For every character in your poetry, you will want to know their favourite food, favourite song or album, their greatest fear, their biggest regret, and so on. This can work even if the character is based on a real person, such as your grandfather. If he has died and you cannot find out what his favourite song was, decide for him. In this way, you will be writing a person, rather than a stereotype or phantom.

When you have written a character or persona poem about an experience that is different to your own, please do not rush to launch it into the world. Show it to someone you trust, ideally someone with the lived experience you have written about or a greater knowledge of it than you. Be prepared to be challenged and criticised by them, listen to their feedback and be grateful for it. If they point out problematic parts in what you have written, don't get defensive – they actually do know better than you – be humble and ask for suggestions as to how you can fix it. Re-draft until you get it right. Get second, third and fourth opinions until you are satisfied you have successfully done what you set out to do. Then, and only then, you will be ready to publish or perform your character or persona poem. No matter how noble your intentions, it's far better to spend a long time working on a good poem than a lifetime apologising for or regretting a poorly executed one.

Creating Unfaithful Beauties: On Translating Poems

Clare Pollard

I have been a writer since I can remember. There are few things I find more pleasurable than hours spent moving words around: switching verbs, cutting adjectives, adding commas. But I also feel strongly that a good poem should be *necessary*. It should express an original thought or unarticulated experience, or make us see things in an unfamiliar way. No one, or no one I've ever met at least, is brilliant enough to sit at their desk every day and conjure up something vital and utterly new. On those days I have the urge to write but not the inspiration, I remember that there is something else I have always been too: an avid reader. I go to my laptop in service of other writers that I love. I edit, I review, I blog, I blurb, and best of all, I translate.

It is perhaps strange that translation has become such a large part of my writing life. It feels a great privilege to be involved in the world of translation at all, as I'm not a linguist. French was the only GCSE I didn't get an A+ in, despite all my revision. Because of this I was advised for the sake of my university applications not to pursue a language at A-Level. I have no aural memory and terrible problems with pronunciation (my husband expressed disbelief when I became editor of *Modern Poetry in Translation*, noting that I can't even pronounce jalapeno correctly.) I must confess I got deep into my twenties barely reading any translated poetry, let alone thinking that I'd ever be permitted to translate myself. And a lot of poetry lovers feel like that – that translated poetry is somehow too difficult, too inaccessible, not for them and they don't know where to begin.

I was finally given permission to translate myself thanks to a British Council trip to Hungary, where I spent time with a group of young Hungarian poets who translated voraciously as part of their poetic practice, particularly Anna Szabo, who became a great friend and collaborator. I was paired with her at the translator's house on Lake Balaton, and she gave me what was called a 'literal' translation of her work – there is much debate over which term to use, with many people now preferring 'bridge', but it was basically a very rough word-for-word translation she had made. Anna then read me the original and answered my questions about form, music and meaning. We had a pile of Hungarian dictionaries to hand. I set to work and loved it.

What are the pleasures of translation? In some ways translating involves being an enthusiastic reader and fan – every translation is a new reading of a text, in which you decide what is brilliant and important in the original, and try to replicate it; in which you say: *look what this poet is doing! Look how amazing this is!* If you like close reading, translating is close-reading-plus – a chance to really get down into the nitty gritty of another writer's language. In other ways, it's like doing a puzzle or a word game, trying to make things fit a shape or metre. Early on, you often have to decide what can be sacrificed – do you need to preserve the rhythm, the form, the sound-effects, the lineation, the brevity? (To keep them all is likely to be impossible). Will you err on the side of fidelity, or create what the Hungarians call 'unfaithful beauties'? Can that pun be translated, or must you find its equivalent in English instead?

Then there is friendship: it can involve the chance to get to know a writer with whom you share something (and in my case often co-translators too). If poetry is a vocation that is often lonely, it is a pleasure to make art as a collaborative act. Lydia Davis names one of her pleasures in translation as being that, "you are not as alone as you are when writing your own work." The poet and translator Sophie Collins has proposed that 'intimacy' might be an alternative to 'fidelity' when talking of translation. But as well as closeness there is distance too. Like travel, translation gives us access to the world beyond our own – different politics, philosophies, tastes, smells, views. The amazing, infinite particularity of lives beyond our own experience.

A position of humility

I should say something at this point about the word 'translate'. It means to bear something across. I like this idea, of crossing borderlines, of bearing witness, of the translator as somehow carrying the other – having a responsibility to them. In this way the translator's position, for me, should be one of humility, and I felt that to be particularly true when co-translating the Somali poet Asha Lul Mohamud Yusuf into English for the first time with Said Jama Hussain and Maxamed Xasan Alto. I would never co-translate someone who I didn't think was at least as good or a better poet than myself, and as such I don't have much time for translators who, when they carry a poem into English, also anglicise it, smoothing out mixed metaphors, changing perceived clichés, toning it down, getting rid of repetitions. They often seem to me arrogant.

For Somalis, as a nomadic people, poetry is central to their sense of identity, and though Asha has been in exile in the UK for 20 years and is articulate in English, her poems, which she says are a 'gift from God' still come to her in Somali, and in incredibly complex metrical and alliterative forms which are only possible in Somali. I believe she is one of our great poets, protesting patriarchy and colonialism with astonishing technical mastery. She expands my sense of what poetry can do. If there are aspects of traditional Somali poetry which can seem clumsy to an English ear – the politically charged rhetoric (readers in the UK often loathe the sense they're being told what to think), the length and seeming bagginess, the extreme alliteration (entire poems often alliterate on just one letter), the shifts in address, the digressions – then it is my job to show that these poems are the opposite of clumsy, they just use techniques which are currently deemed 'unfashionable' on Creative Writing courses.

Worry, worry, worry

When translation is loosened, we tend to call that a version. It's often signalled, in poetry, with a subtitle eg 'after Pushkin', 'after Rimbaud'. I've tended to call one of my other books, *Ovid's Heroines*, a version as I don't feel the same responsibility to Ovid as I would to a living writer, or to someone of whom I was the only translator. I've pared the *Heroides* back in places to make it readable, cut a few references and names I thought would be lost on a modern audience. I chose to write it in free verse, with a deliberately anachronistic tone, as I wanted the voices to sound modern. The reality though is that most good translations or versions are actually somewhere in between those two terms – those artificial binaries of translation and version. They are always, as Kate Briggs has it in her wonderful essay *This Little Art*, which I'd highly recommend, 'twice-written', always inevitably new art-works produced by collaboration. Good translators are also filled with care to somehow get it right, the: 'worry worry worry' as Briggs puts it, over 'the difference between this word and that, the weight and angle and sound and even taste of this word over that'.

Some practical things. If you're interested in translation the first thing is to find a text. Antena, a language justice and language experimentation collaborative founded in 2010 by Jen Hofer and John Pluecker, whose 'Manifesto for Ultratranslation' is an exhilarating document I urge you to read, says: 'Who we choose to translate is political.' I have been lucky in that the British Council and Poetry Translation Centre have paired me with poets I have a deep affinity with, but if you're making the decision yourself, think about who you want to translate and why. There are many under-translated female, LGBTQ+, disabled, working class or BAME writers, for example, as well as under-translated parts of the world (I receive few African translations at *MPT*). Whether the world needs another translation of Rilke is a different question.

If the poet has been dead for more than 70 years (like Ovid), the work will be out copyright, which makes things easier. If they are living you need to check that the poet would be happy with you translating the poem(s) – many poets are on social media or have a contact email on their websites, or you could contact their publisher. Poets are usually happy to be translated, whilst being in contact with them has the added advantage that you may be able to ask questions. It is worth knowing that in the UK the copyright of the translation lies with the translator.

Ideally, you are bilingual. If not you may have to think about how you are going to get a bridge or literal translation as a starting point. Are there old translations in existence? Could you use a combination of Google Translate and a dictionary? (this works for some languages more than others). Better, do you know a linguist or native speaker who would be willing to collaborate? If you do find someone willing to help, make sure you are both credited properly as co-translators.

There are lots of great poets right now who are expanding our ideas about what translation is, and exploring other sorts of translation too. Can you translate a poem into dance? A picture into a poem? Can you translate a dream? Can you translate across time? I translated or reworked many old ballads into 21st century versions in my book *Changeling*, with Jack Underwood's reworkings of canonical poems in *Tenuous Rooms* another example. Intra-lingual versioning has become ubiquitous in creative writing workshops, with people often taking an existing poem as a scaffold and reworking it. I think such exercises can be very useful (I have learnt most of my life skills through mimicry) but my advice would be similar to that of publishing an inter-linguistic translation – as a minimum, always make sure you write 'after X' as the subtitle, and if you want to publish it and the author is alive, it might be polite to try and get in touch with them and ask their permission.

It's also worth asking *why* you are making a new version of this text. If it's just a matter of stealing their smart idea, that's fine for practise, but perhaps your version should stay in the drawer. For it to work as a 'twice written' thing you need to be bearing something across – carrying the poem into a new space, whether that means changing place, time, gender, genre, language or something else. To be elevated beyond an exercise, it needs to become its own new thing. Whilst we're on the subject it's also worth saying that allusions are great (I use lots of them), but only work when the reference is recognisable. It's one thing to repurpose the line 'that which we call a rose / By any other name would smell as sweet' from Shakespeare, quite another to use, uncredited, a line you read in a magazine by a contemporary. No one is ever likely to take you to court over plagiarism – the financial stakes are too low and it is very hard to prove – but reputations have certainly been trashed online in recent years, and it pays to be scrupulous and generous. Make sure anyone who has inspired you receives the thanks they deserve. The bottom line is, any translation or 'version' or collage is a collaborative piece of art and all parties should be credited.

Yes, there are potential pitfalls and ethical considerations when translating or versioning any text, but I hope that does not put you off. Translation as a process has become central to my poetic practice. It has meant I always have something to work on, on those mornings I sit at my desk and don't feel inspired; it has brought together my writing and reading selves; it has given me models outside the contemporary UK mainstream that have made me be braver with my own poetry; it has brought me paid work, travel, and friendship. Best of all, it has allowed me the privilege of bringing poets I adore to new audiences. I mean have you read Anna Szabo? The woman is a genius. And Asha Lul Mohamud Yusuf? And Ovid's *Heroides*? If not, this is me fervently pressing them into your hands.

Computer Says "O": On Using Technology in Poetry

Harry Man

Computers are our facilitators and simulators, broadening the idea of what a canvas for a poem looks like. We can choose language from a vast palette of culture, vocabulary, phrase, idiom, address and register and apply them to new two- and three-dimensional surfaces and interactive environments that have previously never been conceived of before. We are incredibly fortunate to be among the first few generations of explorers within this new artistic terrain. Language can be our means, but we are no longer limited to vellum or the page as our material. What follows then are just seven rules of thumb that will help you to explore technology with more confidence and, I hope, will inspire you to craft some new digital creations of your own[23].

We are all beginners

As a data analyst I've worked with coders that can automate two and half million lines of data, no problem, but cannot fathom how to get the sound to work on their TV or get their daughter's LED shoes to light up. Everyone is a beginner, and like learning an instrument, you'll only get better if you play. Using just one app or noodling around on a site like those listed over the page, just a couple of times a month, and setting aside twenty minutes of an evening to just have a play, with no expectations, is perfect. There are also plenty courses available via your local library and online. There are also lots of videos on YouTube and podcasts on the Podcasts app on

---

[23]   I have been a web developer, a publisher, a digital editor, a data analyst and a poet, and I have been writing code for around 20 years, These rules come from what people have asked me in the past, and I hope they will be useful for you.

your phone, Spotify, Stitcher, etc., that can get you started with both internet-enabled devices and digital literature. Sites like The Literary Platform and Code Academy will also help you on your journey. The sooner you start, the less marooned and the more confident you'll feel as time goes on.

Read what you know and read what you'd throw

Simon Armitage has said in the past that writer's block was the condition of having nothing to say; I believe it's a condition of having nothing to read. Reading works via stealth, to inform, to vanquish your preconceptions and inspire your own writing. To that end, the Electronic Literature Organization has a superb archive. If more experimental literature is your bag, then take a look at UbuWeb which has a mixture of visual poetry and electronic literature from throughout the twentieth and twenty-first centuries, from Hannah Hoch's extraordinary pre-punk Dadaist collages to Cia Rinne's startling visual poems, to interviews with the likes of choreographer Merce Cunningham and a rather inebriated Philip K. Dick. Reading what you don't like is as useful as reading what you do like. You'll pick up techniques and skills that are alien to you and that will suddenly speak to you as your appetites and acumen change. I keep a shelf of poetry collections and bookmark poems I struggle with for exactly this purpose and I'm forever glad for some of the poets I've rediscovered as a result. As corny as it might sound, I think that reading with an open heart is what keeps all of us more open.

For everyone, rejection is proof of hard labour

This is more of a sanity check, than strictly advice. As on paper, so on screen, getting rejected is part of the job, but it's not just a pain that *you* suffer alone. Every poet suffers, no matter the number of awards they've won or what their CV or their latest social media update says. It's often said among the security services, their successes are private and their failures are public, where for poets the inverse is true; our failures are private but our successes are public. This means that what we see of other's success is completely disproportionately high, so to coin a phrase, while we're here, let's celebrate. The time and place for your writing will come your way too and when it does, you'll feel even more able to enjoy it.

Social media is divisional by design

Big social media platforms make their money by encouraging you to return again and again to their site. If you're in a tangle with someone online, that's exactly what you'll do and you'll make Mark Zuckerberg even more rich in the process. If Facebook is making your comment easy to misinterpret, then it's making money. Reduce your anxiety and increase your writing time by sticking to pages and groups that are designed to offer practical advice and reading lists. The Royal Literary Fund has a lot of Facebook groups filled with writing advice, primarily geared toward essay writing, but that can be very helpful for writers of any discipline. If you're genuinely interested in changing minds, then check out Change My View. It's a thread on Reddit, that is filled with people who are there for that purpose.

The goal is not to be published, but to be published well

You will always need a human editor and once whatever you've created is ready to be published, you should be thinking about a timetable for either its deletion, or how you intend to archive that material. This is what the generation after mine have termed 'curation' and when writing online, the minute you publish something, it's part of the bargain. Keeping an archive will help other people (particularly your family and friends as well as critics, academics and the wider readership) to read your work easily after you've moved on.

If it's published online, is it published? Answer: Yes

As much it pains me to say it, the answer is in the question. If you write poetry, you really should try and stick to the rule that if it's published online, it's published. As somebody that writes poetry, just as I would for a physical journal, I would try and share drafts either in person, over email, via Skype or over the phone, the feedback's faster and more honest and it saves you having to think about this question any more.

Instapoetry is a reason to be cheerful

No doubt you'll have seen and perhaps even experimented with creating your own instapoetry. It's hard to adequately measure an instapoem's effectiveness when it is stripped of its surrounding images of sun-kissed beaches, friends in their most flattering light on holiday, or celebrities clutching their awards or engaged in drought-relief. The sense of 'where did it all go wrong' for the average Instagram user must be crushing. It's little wonder that the poem telling you that someone out there "could never have known it when they took you for granted" is garnering more likes than anything else on the platform. Sometimes instapoets in this way are performing, what many teenagers would see as a public service and, as much as it pains us old formalists, one that side-steps our received wisdom of how poetry forms work. At the same time, among the largely wonky, mis-spelled aphorisms and occasion-specific maxims of instapoetry, there is continuation of a very ancient poetry tradition that goes all the way back to Horace's view that poetry should "either instruct or delight". Instapoetry's craft is in its hashtags and the timing of posts, in its similarities to famous quotes, its combinations of backdrops and text, consistency of style and approach, community interaction, keywords and search engine optimisation and how the account makes use of the platform's latest features, which also boost visibility. These elements of an instapoem's craft have usurped a lot of the techniques we're used to seeing, like literary allusion, prosody, attention to rhyme, narrative and metaphor because they are simply harder to absorb in the two or three seconds in which an instapoem is usually consumed. So nobody panic, the instapoem is just as well-crafted, it's just that we can't always see the brushstrokes.

Recommended apps and programmes for your experiments

While these are correct at the time of writing, new apps are being developed all the time while others are no longer maintained, so my apologies in advance if any of these go offline. I've tried to select the most reliable sources that have been around for two or more years for you. If you'd like me to take a look at your digital poetry project or creations, you can tweet them to me or tag me in them on Instagram at @harrymantweets:

Adobe Spark – This is a free photo-editing tool that is useful for instapoems and has some interesting filters templates and fonts that create very professional and slick-looking posts, but it does have a little bit of a learning curve. It's worth trying Quotes Creator first to get a feel for how you like to design, before installing Spark; the latter will direct you to royalty-free images that will save you a hefty image usage fee.

AR Text – Whenever I open this up I think of *Sesame Street*'s old sketch with the pigs dressed as astronauts, 'PIGS IN SPAAACE' and think instead 'TEXT IN SPAAACE'. Yes, it's paid for, which is a pain, but on the plus side, it's one of the best augmented reality (AR) apps I've used for text. You can put text into any space in front of you and add your own effects. You can make videos and adjust the size and appearance of the text easily, and it has yet to crash on me. Apps in a similar realm that are worth investigating include Arrow, Typotastic and Type Art.

Between Page and Screen – Another augmented reality text tool, this time a website (http://www.betweenpageandscreen.com).

You can use it to generate poems that float above QR-code like markers and watch your words float in a satisfying Bladerunner-esque circle. If you're feeling confident after trying this out, you can also develop 'Auras' with an app called HP Reveal. Auras are just a technobabble term for any image that can be scanned with a mobile device that, in so doing, will reveal a piece of text or video underneath. In other words Auras are images or text that are interactive. They can be embedded within images of your choosing which then trigger video, text and other elements. This is a more involved digital format to set up, but nevertheless, filled with hugely exciting potential.

Language is a Virus – Named after the William Burroughs quote, the site (http://www.languageisavirus.com/index.php) contains a huge number of tools, resources and contextual information for experimenting with poems including a visual poetry tool that allows you to draw shapes that are then filled with your choice of text.

Markov Chain Text Generator – This is a small sandbox (testing area) for working with predictive text. You can type in phrases from poems and the generator will then return its own synthesised phrases. It is the poetry equivalent to the deep-fake, here: https://projects.haykranen.nl/markov/demo/

Poetry Pin – A wonderful poetry-come-treasure-hunt project pioneered by Christopher Jelley. Here you can explore poetry trails that Jelley has created around the South West of England. https://www.poetrypin.info

Quotes Creator – This is an app for iOS and Android and the perfect place to start for writing your own instapoems. The free version has a watermark, and the paid 'pro' version is £3.99 at the time of writing. You can easily write your own short aphorisms and post them quickly to Instagram. Remember to put together a list of hashtags for your work before you post it up, to get the best response for your audience.

QR Code Generator – QR codes are small pixelated boxes that you can scan with your phone. I've written poems that use them allowing readers to look out over the surface of the Earth or find out information pertinent to the poem without having to use a footnote or an epigraph. Having used tracking links to see how often people will use them, even on something like a commercial flyer, it's distressingly few, but at the same time, it's a nice gesture. You can find lots of QR code generators online, I use https://www.qr-code-generator.com and you can track your links using bit.ly (www.bit.ly).

There is No Closing Time:
On the Poetics of Performance

Joelle Taylor

*"to speak of the poem in performance is... to overthrow the idea
of the poem as a fixed, stable, finite linguistic object"*
– Charles Bernstein, *Close Listening (1998).*

The craft of performing poetry is concerned with connection. It tells us that poetry is a verb.

Spoken word[24] is pre-literate in origin, an expression of oral-based cultures globally. It is many things, but it is not 'the new rock and roll'. In some ways, rock and roll was the new poetry. Neither does spoken word find its origins in hip hop, though that has contributed to the development of some artists, as has jazz, punk and reggae sound systems. It is as old as the tongue.

In contemporary culture, spoken word is an effective method of bypassing literary gatekeepers and directly connecting with an audience and prospective readership. To perform a poem in this way is a political act irrespective of the content of the piece. As a consequence, the art attracts more people from marginalised communities[25] with limited cultural access than those from more privileged strata. The art is bound with the politics of class, race and gender and offers rich potential because of that. Events become seeding grounds for new thinking, and radical resistance. I often think of underground poetry and spoken word as the last free art: there are no 'Open

---

24   'Spoken word', 'performance poetry', 'underground poetry', and
        'spoken word poetry' are used interchangeably throughout this essay.
        Each refers to a poet whose primary practice is in the performance of
        their poems.
25   'Marginalised communities' includes working-class, black, Asian,
        minority ethnic, D/deaf or disabled, and LGBT people.

Walls' in galleries or 'Open Stages' in theatres to complement the Open Mic, and we might find it strange that a ballet is preceded by local ballerinas having five minutes each. But the Open Mic is the birthing ground of spoken word.

I found my voice stuffed down the back of an old microphone in a Lancashire working-man's club in the mid 1980s. Like most performance poets of that time I did not have my own space with a specific audience, but would play support to bands or be a part of a political demonstration. This led to a style in performance poetry that was elevated, loud and attention grabbing; a necessary evolution when attempting to speak to 50 people who just turned to the bar as you were introduced. Only in recent years have we acquired distinct spaces for spoken word poetry and this semantic has once again pushed the art to develop.

There is a diverse range of performance in poetry, from full physical possession, to minimal and still. Spoken word poetry is surreal, political, comedic, enraged, grief-struck, gentle and incisive. It is musical, epic, intimate and theatrical. It has roots in music, liturgy, storytelling and political oratory. In other words, at its best, performance poetry is sensuous, employing the full spectrum of the human emotional condition. Authenticity is a key word in the art. When dissected 'authentic' invariably means 'working class'. The use of the pronoun 'I' in spoken word is prevalent. This fits with the notion of authenticity within the work; it is rare that a performance-based poet speaks of something they have not directly experienced. These poets speak from their lives rather than of them. There is an intimacy to even the most furious of performances, a slightly parted door.

Rather than the last layer of a poem, performance itself is a poetic. The poems are written with the mouth with a live and present audience in mind. It considers the audience. It considers the idea of response and how that will affect the piece. A performance veers from the page in crucial ways. The first is that a performance is never the same, it is fleeting and transitory. Spoken word occupies liminal space. It is a moment, and as such unrepeatable. In spoken word, a poem is not completed until it is performed; the audience occupying the role of its final editor.

As soon as your name is called

I often tell students that their performance begins as soon as their name is called, and that the walk to the stage is as important as their first words on it. This is partially true. In fact, the performance begins before the audience has even entered the space. The semantics of venue are crucial and determine the way in which poetry or a poet are received. The same poet can perform the same poems in the back room of a bar or in the main space of the Queen Elizabeth Hall and have completely different responses. That is not only due to the fact that different venues attract different demographics, but that the space itself says something to the audience as they enter.

A back-room bar tells the audience that what they are about to see is working class, that they can be more liberal in their responses, freer perhaps, and that alcohol is an expected part of the night. The main space in a prestigious venue tells the audience they are about to see and listen to something important, something with weight. However, those prestigious venues can also overwhelm an audience, so that they become afraid of their own hands, unsure of when to applaud, which can alter the intended energy of an evening. And it is worth noting that mainstream media and critics will rarely attend the pub reading, even if the same poets are programmed.

Performance is a dynamic exchange between the audience and the poet; it is not static or fixed. But as more spoken word artists are finding publishers (such as Burning Eye Books, a cultural revolution in its own right) we cannot ignore the profound effect it has on the underground poet to see their words published, and for that to be a market for their work. This has to have an impact on the writing itself for the genre to evolve.

The written poem is the first script and the performance its second. On stage you will do all your workings out on your face as though it is a page. Performance is not acting. It is *remembering*. By this, I don't mean memorisation, but that it is the returning to the dynamic space in which the poem was written – or the subject of the piece – and reproducing the energy that provoked the writing. In other words, the body is authentic rather than choreographed. In spite of this you will find that you begin to make the same movements whenever you perform the same poem, and this can aid memorisation. You embody the poem, allow it to become a part of you, or to return to where it began. But those movements must first come from you, who you are. I move my arms and hands a lot on stage, partly because my heritage is from a long line of cotton mill workers, who tried to talk over the deafening looms and resorted instead to an increased use of gesture to communicate; this is common among Lancashire women of my generation, as is the use of wide facial expressions. It is also a technique I became aware of using more in schools, when visually trying to explain what certain words or ideas in poems meant. Don't do it if that is not you. Stillness is as important as movement.

We must all pay attention to vectors though. Vectors are the lines the body create in movement; they direct attention, and effect emotion. For example, a curled-in body and lowered head suggests what is about to be said isn't that important. Worse still, it makes an audience think more about the poet than the poem. There is also something to be considered around the biology of performance, how having a living organism emit sound waves at someone affects their brain receptors and emotional centre. We are all made of water, and water moves to audio waves.

We cannot do much to alter the way we speak but with thought and vocal exercises we can deepen tone, monitor speed and adjust to fit movements in the poem, and maintain a consistent volume. Our relationship to music means that the spoken word artist must consider the voice as a part of the piece; it is a musical instrument, as well as the tool you use to dig out words.

There are some clear vocal patterns at work in popular live poetry and whilst these lend a musicality that can attract audiences, overuse of these patterns can eliminate the poem itself. The first thing I do when a new Button Poetry[26] video drops with that recognisable and often repeated pattern is to turn the sound off and read the words. This style is evangelical, it seeks to inspire an audience to its feet. It is a victory poem. This is a worthy art but so often repeated and superimposed on pieces of work that do not naturally fall into that rhythm that I have become cautious of it. It feels like artifice – the exact opposite of what spoken word can offer. But the development of poetic cadence is fundamental to the writing of spoken word. The difficulty is in finding the pattern that is unique to each poet, a true reflection of both the work and the writer.

Evolution in the poetry underground

Finally, I want to return briefly to the notion of how the publication of spoken word artists must have a role in evolving the art form.

We are at an interesting moment in the UK, a bridge between two fiercely separated expressions of the same form. Poets who write exclusively for the page have learned from watching the explosion in popularity of spoken word, the way the artist connects with an audience, and are learning their pieces. Equally, spoken word artists are both reading and writing more books, and evolving their written word as a consequence.

---

26   https://buttonpoetry.com/

Club bookings reflect this with the best nights programming both the best in spoken word alongside those of the page. A book written by a spoken word artist must use the media effectively and explore all the boundaries and possibilities of the page. A book offers more potential than just being the sleeve lyrics to an album. A book endures. There is no closing time. We should be inspired by those US poets who made their name on the slam circuit, such as Patricia Smith, Danez Smith and sam sax, who have gone on to write award-winning collections and been accepted into the literary establishment. We are in an unusual position in which we can challenge page form and can seek to apply performance to the page in new and innovative ways.

What might impede us is in the UK is the class system and the lack of consistent infrastructure to support the development of working-class writers, during the transition from performed to written word. There is no reason why a poet cannot work effectively and powerfully in both live and printed media. The book itself is a kind of performance.

But how can a scene evolve when it is consistently exiled from the cultural mainstream? Where are the UK versions of Def Poetry Jam[27], or the televised late-night spoken word club? A spoken word poet will rarely, if ever, have their event reviewed in *The Guardian* or *London Review of Books*, and so the art created its own critical arena: the poetry slam. Here poets who may not be published or have access to literary platforms get both to put their work in the world and elicit immediate critical response in the form of points, sometimes with feedback. The poetry slam is our *Times Literary Supplement*. Even so we still need to develop the tools with which to effectively review live poetry performances; I dream of a time when the art is considered equal to the literary canon and shares the same column inches in review sections. But let us be clear that 'marginalised' is a

---

27   Def Poetry Jam – a popular US television series hosted by Mos Def

synonym for 'less-than', and poets from those communities will struggle to have their works valued in the same way as published materials. And yet still we continue: connecting, writing on air, and editing with our mouths.

In these dystopian times it has never been more important for a poet, live or page-based, to perform their work, to interact with audiences and forge both cultural and political connections. I call it the poetry underground because there is some form of shelter there. To write a poem is an act of resistance, to perform it a revolution.

PART FOUR

WHERE POETIC CRAFT
MEETS REAL LIFE

Beyond the Known:
On Using Research in Your Poetry

Roy McFarlane

You have this idea for your next collection, pamphlet or poems and you suddenly realise you've got to go and research. Where do you begin? How much time do you dedicate to researching? And how do you create the alchemy of poetry, out of all that material?

In writing my poetry collection *The Healing Next Time*, I wanted to write a poem about Mark Duggan[28] in response to reading Claudia Rankine's *Citizen*. I envisioned creating one particular story around 'The Activist' with all his flaws, fighting racism in a post-Stephen Lawrence Inquiry Britain. But, in the end, the core of the collection found its beating heart in the 18 sonnets about deaths in custody. I couldn't run from the truth of families and individuals encountering, then dying at the hands of the state – the police, the prison system and mental health institutions.

There was an urgency to write these buried stories, often lost in bureaucracy and cover-ups, and families worn out by the lies and failures of a system set against them, and this became the emotional connection that drove me to tackle the subject. Passion ties you in for the long run, the long days of researching, searching for a needle of poetry in a haystack of reports and information.

It's important to have an idea of your subject. I've been involved in anti-racism and community work from the 1990s and have participated in the marches, sat in on the inquests. I was aware of *Dying for Justice*, edited by Harmit Athwal and

---

28   Mark Duggan, a 29-year-old British man, was shot and killed by police in Tottenham, North London on 4 August 2011. For more see: https://en.wikipedia.org/wiki/Death_of_Mark_Duggan

Jenny Bourne, published by the Institute for Race Relations (IRR), and an earlier publication written over 20 years before, *Deadly Silence: Black Deaths In Custody*. Having read these publications, I needed to contact Harmit and share with her my ideas for my new collection. Harmit was more than willing to help and let me see the material that the IRR had amassed over the last 50 years.

Immersion and inhabiting

Building a good relationship with an organisation or an individual is a good way to start. It requires you to be clear about your objectives, showing the utmost respect to the subject and all those concerned. I willingly read poems for a conference on migration hosted by the IRR, to facilitate better relationships with them. Building these relationships can give you something fresh, something new via conversations and behind-the-scenes knowledge, shedding light on hidden gems that you'll never find in the articles.

Over a period of a year I immersed myself in the IRR's files of deaths in custody from 1969 to the present day. Shelves upon shelves, box files upon box files and wallets with the names of individuals written in the corner. I picked files at random and spread newspaper reports, flyers, posters, and inquest reports, across a table and read or waited for something to inhabit me. I watched countless documentaries, short films and YouTube material.

All that was needed, at this stage, to kickstart the process, was one line or a voice jumping off the page, and notes would start flying into my notebook. On other occasions, I could cross reference materials. 'Mark Duggan 2011' took the longest time to formulate; documentaries, news reports, interviews and photographs, all merged into pages and pages until I read this quote by a community activist: "He wasn't an angel, anything else and you won't survive."

Cold stare into a white page

There's a silence when you're faced with white space on the page. How do you turn a research into a narrative, a piece of prose or a poem? How do you find a way of merging reader (witness) and victim together, with the hope of moving from a report or historical account, to a place where the reader is touched, leading them to experience the tragedy, the pain lying beneath the narrative? Sometimes you find a line like "they killed him" in Clinton McCurbin, or the raw image of a man lying in a hospital bed linked to a life support machine, as with the poster of Brian Douglas. The report and released footage of the pursuit of Azelle Rodney and his final moments is the shortest sonnet in my collection, but it mirrors the pursuit and firing of weapons.

It's this handling of the truth that I believe is a creative power to harness in our writing. The muse pushes us to the edge, to write the truth. That cold stare into the white page and, out of it, writing our emotional truth.

As poets we're not here to write some empirical truth. But it's the energy that breaks the realms of conformity, leaping over barriers of safety into the void of the unknown. Truth is relative to the writer, and the reader brings their truth to the reading – but we find a common ground within poetry, when it works.

I kept returning to Tyehimba Jess, re-reading his Pulitzer Prize winning book, *Olio*[29]. It's a tour de force, taking up the mantle of making poetry that witnesses the past; the inventiveness and the imagination to look at white space and create the most magically-shaped poems. To grab different forms of writing such as prose, reports, dialogue, sonnets and concrete poems to create a masterpiece that reflects the times we're living in.

Olio is full of improvisation and plays with form, dialogue, reportage, negro spirituals and interviews. Take 'Pre/Face Berryman/Brown' for example:

---

29   Published by Wave Books, 2016.

The poem then,	Let me say
Whatever its wide cast of characters,	despite loss… I won my life. This story –
Is essentially about	how a slave steals back his skin:
An imaginary character	smuggles loose like I did. It lives on,
(not the poet,	but through words – and
Not me)	free. I'm

On the left we find the italicised text excerpted from John Berryman's introductory note to *The Dream Songs*; on the right is Mr. Henry "Box" Brown who slipped from slavery by mailing himself free to Philadelphia, who returns many years later to play a part in John Berryman's *Dream Songs*. Here we have the found text italicised alongside the voice of Brown with the minimal of space in-between, to show difference, but close enough to keep that conversation, and to highlight the dichotomy: white/black, writer/actor, the imagined/the real.

The writing of 'David Bennett, 1998' and 'Mark Duggan, 2011' was inspired by the work of Jess. Start with David. In one of the reports, I found a reference to a letter which he had sent to the Head of Nursing Services in the clinic where he was being treated[30], which got me thinking about the last moments before he died. I tried to write a piece that mirrored his well-articulated letter against the imagined anger of a man fighting for his life. I tried the following:

David Bennett, 1998

as you know	the world's against me
black boys in this clinic	wanting to make a phone call
I don't know if you realised	another patient using the phone
there are no Africans	'black bastard, you niggers…'
on your staff at the moment.	Nothing is done after they fight
We feel	he feels
there should be at least	something should be done
two black persons	to the other guy.

---

30   NSC NHS Strategic Health Authority (2003) Independent Inquiry into the death of David Bennett.

in the medical or social work staff.	His sister is all that he wants
For the obvious reasons	he's separated and moved
security and contentment	punches a female nurse in the jaw
for all concerned	he's pinned face down
please do your best	they've released him
to remedy this appalling situation	realising he'd stopped breathing.

I focused on mirroring the lines as closely as possible, keeping most of the written letter and breaking the line where it felt natural, followed closely by the events that led to his death, found in the report. Here the conversations are in conflict with each other, and I was happy – for me it showed what happens when the oppressed try to articulate their concerns and the reality of what really happens when you're ignored.

But I had to continually bear in mind how we naturally read from left to right, as well as reading down the two columns. When reading it again, most of the lines failed in creating this conversation. I tried to rewrite it, tried to make the two sides communicate, but struggled; the italicised text refused to be changed and the voice of those last moments refused to lose its urgency. So I tried the following:

David Bennett, 1998

As you know there are
black boys in this clinic.
I don't know if you realized
there are no Africans
on your staff at the moment.
We feel
there should be at least
two black persons
in the medical or social work staff.
For the obvious reasons
security and contentment
for all concerned
please do your best

to remedy this appalling situation.
The world's against him

> he wants to make a phone call
> another patient using the phone
> 'black bastard, you niggers...'
> Nothing is done after they fight
> he feels
> something should be done
> to the other guy.
> His sister is all that he wants
> he's separated and moved
> punches a female nurse in the jaw
> he's pinned face down
> they've released him
> realising he'd stopped breathing.

Here, both voices jostle for position within the white spaces, almost like there should be a response, but they're on their own whilst being aware of each other.

When starting to think about how to approach 'Mark Duggan 2011', I returned to Jess, noting his use of researched material and poetic talk. He ventures a step beyond, taking dual voices and playing with the possibility of cross-talk in 'Coon songs must go! / Coon songs go on [2]':

In this way	I make cash –
and in many other ways	I give white folks giggle
too numerous to mention	when I wear blackface. Yeah, them
"coon" songs	
have done more	earnin' much bread. Want
to insult the	highfalutin'
Negro and cause	hilarity with

Jess juxtaposes the dilemma of the insult and the harm of the coon songs, brought to the black community, along with the necessity to make a living to survive. The songs bridge that dilemma.

In my poem I tried something similar, influenced not only by the above poem, but another by Jess called 'Millie and Christie Mckoy', a butterfly-shaped poem about the conjoined twins born into slavery.

Mark Duggan 2011

He wasn't an angel anything else and you won't survive

Murdered   Survived

Because there are very few angels on Broadwater Farm

Planning an attack   Just transporting

In possession of a firearm

One of Britain's most violent gangsters   a son, father, brother & multiple partners

being followed, tyres screeching, officers shouting

He's reaching, he's reaching   He's raising his hands holding a phone

two shots in the arm & chest   a plume of feathers filling the air

He was no angel

holding a gun, throwing it away   not holding a gun, hands held high

a gun was found on the green   nobody saw the gun fly away

the gun in the black sock

There are no angels to be found

in the shadows of the death of PC Blakelock.

The found text "he wasn't an angel" was my point of reference to return to, but when looking at Duggan I wanted to tell the story of the player, father and son against the demonised gangster and lawless individual painted by the police and the media. Two narratives running side-by-side, sharing the same truths at certain points, and then diverging. Although there's not much speech found in this poem, the voices of the police, the community and the haunting voice of PC Blakelock are evoked and sing from the page.

Into the unknown

Both these poems started in research, in reality, but only came to life by heading into the unknown, into what I didn't know;

that's how you get to the truth. As Selima Hill once said, "There is no other way but through. You can't go over it. You can't go under it. You've got to go through it! Go naked into the shower of truth."

Of Guardians and Destroyers: On Using Your Family in Your Poetry

Julia Webb

Beyond one to one

Most people when they write poetry about the family – their own, perhaps others – tend to write about the relationship between two family members – mother/son, father/son, sister/ sister etc. What interests me more is wider family dynamics – how the group acts as a whole, how they treat each other, what the power structures within it are and how they shift over time.

Psychologist Murray Bowen's 'Family Systems' theory states that:

> a family functions as a system wherein each member plays a specific role and must follow certain rules. Based on the roles within the system, people are expected to interact with and respond to one another in a certain way. Patterns develop within the system, and each member's behaviors impact the other members in predictable ways. Depending on the specific system, these behavioral patterns can lead to either balance or dysfunction of the system – or both, at various points in time.[31]

According to this theory, even when a person is apart or disconnected from their family emotionally or geographically, the influence of the family still has a profound impact on their emotions, actions, and influences what choices they make.

We are an increasingly mobile society, so it is little surprise that the modern family unit has become spread out geographically

---

31   https://www.regain.us/advice/family/family-systems-theory-definition-what-is-it/

with many adults located far from parents, siblings, and their hometowns. Growing families are often insular, disconnected, without the safety net of an extended family network to fall back on in times of hardship. Given this lack of unconditional support it is hardly surprising that modern nuclear families often become inward looking and make up rituals, rules and coping mechanisms all of their own. I am fascinated by how groups of humans interact with one another – the family particularly because (for most of us) it does have such far-reaching effects – the family as guardian and destroyer. "We look for understanding of the human condition in poetry," says poet Martin Figura and (good) writing about personal experience and the family can give us exactly that.

Getting started

In early drafts it's important not to worry about offending. At this stage, it's more important to get stuff down on the page – you can worry about editing and content later. There are many ways to access memories – an exercise I often use with students is a memory mining exercise based on the book *I Remember* by Joe Brainard. Free write for around 10 minutes starting each sentence with the phrase 'I remember.' This is a great way to harvest ideas that you might want to expand on later. Robert Seatter wrote a similar shorter poem which starts "I come from…" and this phrase works well as a jumping off point too.[32] Remember – if you use any of these lists as your final poem, you will need to acknowledge the source of inspiration – a simple 'after Joe Brainard' or 'after Robert Seatter' under the title would suffice.

When you are starting out you might find that you write quite a few 'anecdote' poems. When I first started writing seriously I wrote a lot of pen portraits and narrative poems about things that had happened in my childhood. Most of these poems did

---

32   The Robert Seatter poem is suggested by Ann Sansom in 'Using What We Know', *The Poetry Toolkit*, (The Poetry Trust, 2010), p13-14

not make it into my first collection because, as one of my MA tutors said, they were 'relentlessly personal.' What he meant was that they described an incident or situation, but were not offering the reader a way into the poem – or a chance to make it their own.

I have read a lot of these types of anecdotal (some quite harrowing) poems, especially in first collections, but I rarely want to revisit them. To draw a reader back a poem has to be doing something other than simply recounting an experience, whether good or bad, and it should avoid telling the reader what to feel or think. You don't have to spell things out for your reader or feel that if you are writing about something based on true experience you have to lever in every little detail for the sake of 'authenticity'. Quoting Figura again:

> People are often more interested in sharing their sadness and anger, than in poetry. It isn't surprising that their poems don't resonate beyond family, friends and support groups. People read poetry because they like poetry, they won't get your story unless it interests them as poetry first.[33]

I had to write those overly personal poems, despite the fact that they stayed mostly on my laptop. Writing them was cathartic, and once I had got them out of my system the way was clear for me to be able to come at my subject matter in more interesting and playful ways.

Metaphor

Using metaphor in family (and relationship) poems is a great way to remove yourself from the situation and to make your subject matter more universal and accessible. It can also be a powerful tool for confronting difficult subject matter – as in 'My Father's City' by Pascale Petit where her sick father becomes Paris:

---

33   Martin Figura, 'Everybody Knows the Troubles I've Seen', *In Their Own Words*, ed. Helen Ivory and George Szirtes, (Salt, 2012), p164

The Jardin des Plantes locks its enclosures
as I dry the garden of your chest.

The winged ghouls of Notre Dame crouch
on your shoulders as you sleep;[34]

Metaphor allows us to write about family matters without upsetting our families too much (unless they are poets of course). I have made my family members into owls, sparrows, circus performers, ghosts, supermarkets and mythological beings, amongst other things.

Metaphor can provide a good way into writing about loss too. Again you might have to write some poems dealing with the practicalities and the raw emotion before you are able to write about the loss in more surprising ways. In my first book there are a couple of poems dealing with the practicalities around losing my mother, but distance has allowed me to look at the situation more objectively. In my second collection *Threat*, I deal in different ways with her loss and the complex emotions that arise around a parent becoming ill and dying – I was even able to imagine different scenarios for bringing her back to life. Alice Willitts beautifully sums up the complexity of feeling about loss in her pamphlet *Dear,*

I've made you
vanish but I want
you back but I don't
be dead
stay dead
better dead[35]

You might find that some losses are more difficult to write about than others because of (amongst other things) the nature of particular family relationships and the circumstances in which the person lived/died. I was able to write about my mother relatively quickly after her death, however, it took me

34   from *Zoo Father* (Bloodaxe, 2001)
35   from *Dear* (Magma, 2019)

more than ten years to be able to write anything at all about the loss of my brother.

Mythologising

A step on from metaphor, requisitioning existing mythology or creating your own, can provide you with the distance needed to write.

My sequence 'Family Values' uses this technique. I created mythological sounding characters – Sun Daddy, Moon Mother and The Star Children – and I fleshed the sequence out with a mixture of personal anecdote, fiction and concrete details from my own childhood. Toon Tellegen does this in *Raptors* and he cleverly flags up that this is what he is doing by way of an introduction by an unreliable narrator who immediately sets the tone for the rest of the book:

> Years ago I invented someone whom I called my father. It was morning, very early, I couldn't sleep any more, I remember it quite clearly. My father didn't seem surprised at having suddenly appeared out of nowhere and, in his turn, invented my mother, my brothers and myself.[36]

In essence he recreates the complexity of family interactions and the way that family memories and stories are changed and manipulated – mythologised – through the telling and retelling of them: who doesn't have an instance where a family member remembers something differently to them? *Raptors* might or might not be based on Tellegen's own family, but what matters is that it is convincing reading; it carries its own truth.

Mixing fact and fiction

There is a liberation in the writing process that allows one to go beyond what is real. I think of a poem as a tiny work of fiction, but that doesn't mean that it can't be based on something

---

36   from *Raptors* (Carcanet, 2011)

true. One of the most common problems in workshops is that students get hung up about not changing things or leaving details out. If you are writing about real events and are hugely attached to the backstory and all the attendant details, then perhaps memoir might be a better medium.

Of course some of my poems *are* based on real events and others are not. Changing or losing some of the details of a real-life event can make it more believable as a poem – I always argue that it is the 'truth of the poem' that matters rather than the 'actual truth'. If something actually happened but it makes the poem feel less true then it's better to lose it. Similarly in my fictional poems I use concrete details from my own childhood, expanding and changing events to suit the needs of the poem. Think about what is interesting about your particular family – what are its quirks and idiosyncrasies? Do you have invented words or rituals?[37] These are the little things that make a poem more believable.

Seeing things from a different perspective

It can be useful when writing about something painful or difficult to try and imagine things from the other person's perspective. I found a way into writing about the loss of my brother, who had mental health issues, by imagining what life might have been like for him, rather than starting from the point of how his problems and loss affected me. Do this as imaginatively as you can and be really specific rather than vague. My poem 'Oh Brother' would have been less interesting if I had written "what was it like to hate being touched?" instead of "did sirens blare when anything touched your skin?" Be bold, be brave.

Multiple perspectives

When I am writing about family I like to explore the idea of what a particular family member could or should be. Take a mother

---

37   My family, for example, used to always have taramasalta on crumpets every Saturday when mum got back from shopping.

for example – what are society's expectations of what a mother should be? What are yours? How should a mother behave? How many different types of mother are there? How many can you invent? The beauty of poetry is that you can invent the family you want, or reimagine the one you have. Carrie Etter does this beautifully in her book *Imagined Sons*, where she imagines over and over what the son that she gave up for adoption at birth might be doing and what he might be like.

Depersonalisation

Another technique I find useful is to depersonalise my characters by not using their given names. Using titles such as 'sister' or 'brother' allows the reader more easily into the poem than 'Neil' or 'Heather' might, and it allows the reader to transpose their own sister or brother onto the poem if they wish. Generic names like Mr Smith or Mrs Grey also work well, as does giving people fictional names that suit their personalities, as in Stevie Smith's poem 'House of Mercy':

> Now I am old I tend my mother's sister
> The noble aunt who so long tended us,
> Faithful and True her name is. Tranquil.[38]

The sticky question of ethics

Of course the biggest pitfall of writing about your family is that you might hurt or offend them – it is best (for both you and your publisher) not to put anything libelous in your poems, but it is up to you to decide exactly how much truth to reveal.

A lot depends on whether the people you are writing about are alive, whether they will read your book and how much you care about how they are affected. I recently read a post on social media that advocated being cautious about everything you write – personally I prefer not to censor my creative process in

---

38   Stevie Smith, *Selected Poems* (Penguin Classics, 2002)

that way, but I certainly don't publish everything that I write (and I did warn my dad that I had taken aspects of our life and fictionalised them). I am not generally as explicitly revelatory about my actual family as, say, Sharon Olds – but like Olds, my poems are factual to differing degrees and I do not consider them confessional:

> Poems like mine – I don't call them confessional, with that tone of admitting to wrong-doing. My poems have done more accusing than admitting. I call work like mine 'apparently personal'. Or in my case apparently very personal.[39]
>
> – Sharon Olds

---

39   'Olds' worlds', *The Guardian*, 26th July 2008

Agents of Change:
On Power, Politics and Class in Poetry

Peter Raynard

"I have not been able to touch the destruction/ within me./ But unless I learn to use/ the difference between poetry and rhetoric/ my power too will run corrupt as poisonous mould." – Audre Lorde, 'Power'

What would you do if you had no power? What lengths would you stretch to, in order to get back some control of your life? To feed your family. To take back your country (whatever the hell that means)? At the extreme, this may involve stealing food or dealing drugs. In the hands of the powerful, it can lean towards dictatorship. As the poet Carolyn Forché says, "there is nothing that one person will not do to another". Hannah Arendt called it *The Banality of Evil.* No one gives up power lightly.

The definitions of politics and class are the subject of reams of academic articles, and back alley fights. Some believe class only exists in the UK, that there is no such thing in the US for example. But this essay is neither academic nor pugilistic.

In my five years editing Proletarian Poetry, publishing poems of working-class lives, I have defined class, and thus politics as being about wealth and power. And through the prism of power, you will be able write about politics and class.

What it boils down to is human relations. Whether you're a Marxist or a capitalist, creationist or evolutionist, bon viveur or recluse, at some point in life you will bump up against the rough chin of power. Politics is the struggle for that power – resources – between different human beings. And lack of power makes people do the damndest of things, such as voters who rely on EU subsidies voting to Leave because they were sick of being ignored.

Power is "the ability to influence other people, organisations, or states, to act in your interests", and can be divided between 'hard' and 'soft' power:

- **Hard Power**; the threat or actual use of violent force, imposition of sanctions on other countries, exclusion/ expulsion of individuals from your country or organisation.

- **Soft Power**; power exerted by non-violent means – for example freedom of speech and a free press, strong institutions of law, government, and civil society. But culture is particularly important; books, music, theatre, football, bingo, the pub.

Poetry is rich in the ways it addresses power, politics and class (though scanning the pages of mainstream poetry magazines, you may think otherwise). Where to start? The following is a whistle-stop tour of examples, mainly drawn from my online poetry journal, Proletarian Poetry[40].

WORK: Generally, work is where we spend a third of our adult lives, and is a toil-based feeding ground for poetry; from the 'Peasant' poet John Clare, through to the late Philip Levine, Fred Voss, and Martin Hayes. The toll of toil goes on, with many people in work trying to survive below the poverty line. But in Kyle Dargan's poem, 'Two Years from Retirement, my Neighbour Contemplates Canada', he addresses the issue of cheap labour and the elephant in the tool shop, the end of work: "Our world becoming old world. / The new world just a flimsy Babel / tower. /// Our sleeping globe, it dreams this/ one dream of expansion everlasting."

And it is not just the men who write about work. Jane Commane's poem 'The Shop-floor Gospel' goes inside the uncertainty felt by workers both in the 1980s and the present, where either redundancies or potential closure are in the air of shop floor gossip: "Fortune-teller, free agent, / laughter in grubby canteens;/ *Mark my words.* / We're a living museum!/ *There's no future*".

HERITAGE: Class is all about relations (not just your aunt and uncle kind); the interactions between different positions of power. Unless you are related to Jacob Rees Mogg, if you go far enough back you will probably find a 'peasant' in your family – someone who licked the roads clean before going to school. Alison Brackenbury's poem 'Pensioned' takes us back more than a hundred years to tell the story of an unlikely friendship between her grandfather, Frank, a gamekeeper on a large estate in England and a local traveller, Hezekiah Brown:

> a tall man, stately, with one eye.
> The shrapnel took it in the war, the Great War. But he fought on, by
> my grandfather, a gamekeeper
> who would have shot him for a hare.

Kim Moore's poem, 'My People', is about the community she grew up with; the good, bad, and contradictory: "I come from scaffolders and plasterers and shoemakers and carers, the type of carers paid pence per minute to visit an old lady's house. Some of my people have been inside a prison." No class is a monolith.

PLACE: We've all lived on streets, in amongst 'others' and their difference, which all makes for rich pickings in terms of class. My own street had a mix of Irish and English working class, with the occasional academic and the 'weird' bloke on the corner who chased you down the street. Mona Arshi's 'On Ellington Road', is a poem full of characters with different backgrounds and histories, living side by side in that London. "Old man Harvey, with his thick specs and polished shoes shouting trespassers, yet offering us a penny for collecting his waspy pears. / 'Biji', looking old in widow-white, whose soft hands were always stained with turmeric."

Place can also be an expression of aspiration and ambition, sometimes eliciting an inherent snobbery, as shown in Sarah Barnsley's funny poem 'O Pioneers', about when her family moved "to the new house behind / the concrete factory. It was still/ the right side of Rickerscote Road, / where, Mum said, the cuffies lived".

POLITICAL HISTORY: Poets from the get-go wrote about power in all its conniving guises, and contemporary poets continue to carry the cudgel. Matt Duggan's poem 'I, Agitator' is about Wat Tyler who led the Peasant's Revolt. "On horseback I heard jingles of blood coins / like marching death in sacks of human snouts, / bowing to the King's groin / our collector – a man of debt and gout." And Malika Booker's 'Lament for the Assassination of Walter Rodney' is a moving poem about how his family and people of Guyana had "their kingdom ruined."

1: The News

The home was cold;
a mother, brother, sister, sat empty,
guts screwed with news that their father dead.

They say he body parts scatter all across Bent street,
they say like Seth scatter Osiris across black tar.

RANTING AND RHETORIC: From the Liverpool poets, to the ranting poets of the 80s, to today's poets of protest and satire, with poetry against the political establishment, and policies inimical to working people and their families. Tim Wells (aka Teething Wells), through his site, Stand Up and Spit[41], has documented the ne'er do wells of poetry for much of these austerity years. The Red Poets of Wales (now in their 26th year), and publishers such as Smokestack Books and Culture Matters continue to keep that ever-so red flag flying.

But as the old adage goes, a week is a long time in politics, which makes political poetry all the more difficult. It is okay if you are submitting online to a current event, but to go into a book or magazine, the poem needs to have a bit more stamina. However, there are many poets out there holding power to account through poetry. One such vanguard is

---

41   standupandspit.wordpress.com

Poets on the Picket Line, who do as it says on their collection tin; supporting striking workers both with loudhailer poetry and much-needed fundraising.

One tried and tested form of political poetry is satire. This is the main currency of Kevin Higgins, berating the hypocrisy of the modern-day villains of Parliament on both sides of the Irish Sea. "What are they waiting for," he asks in 'Waiting for Boris':

> the archbishops and casino owners
> clutching their bags of cocaine,
> the barman at Wetherspoons eyeing the clock,
> and the little people who live
> in Jacob Rees-Mogg's top hat

ECO-POETRY: Not even that stalwart of poetic themes, 'Nature', can escape the politics of power. That Romantic form that stirred the loins of Wordsworth and his clouds, is now under attack by powerful forces. The planet is burning and a lot of us feel powerless to change that situation. As much as we reuse, recycle and reduce our consumption, it is major corporations and the push for profit, which causes most damage to our fragile ecosystem. US poet laureate Joy Harjo's poem 'Remember' is a beautiful elegy to our precious planet:

> Remember the plants, trees, animal life who all have their
> tribes, their families, their histories, too. Talk to them,
> listen to them. They are alive poems.

And in Carrie Etter's long poem 'Scar', she relates the devastating impact of climate change has on her home state of Illinois, literally causing "tornado / drought / flood / heat wave/ blizzard".

FEMINISM: I'm not going to mansplain here but there are not enough portrayals of working class women in literature, although more recently that is changing. In poetry, we have poets such as Nadia Drews, Jane Burn, Janine Booth, Nafeesa Hamid, Theresa Lola, Julia Webb and Fran Lock. Lock has recently completed a fantastic trilogy on working class women in history. In the poem 'Rag Town Girls see God', there is almost an inverted elegy in its telling of the end of man as represented by the deity:

> There he is, eyes half closed, doing the math of a difficult
> miracle, wrist-wearied, leaning into his swig, his pull of
> smoke. We assume he is God. He reminds us of a man
> we once knew: slender and insulted by life, mixing his
> blessings like strong drink, suicidally agile, tying a nimble
> noose the minute your back was turned.

SEXUALITY is sadly still an area where people are discriminated against. Thankfully poets such as Andrew McMillan, Richard Scott and Dean Atta, are pushing the boundaries of power in poetry to some effect. Toby Campion does this with humour in 'Telling the Lads', while directly challenging their notion of masculinity:

> but I'm not like a gay gay
> you know a vodka cranberry gay
> a here-and-queer gay
> I'm more of just like a here gay
> a steak and ale pie gay.

RESPONDING TO ATROCITY: Whether it is the Holocaust or 9/11, writing after horrific events is both urgent and difficult. How do you find a way into a poem, when such horrors are so all encompassing? Pascale Petit did this with sensitivity and beauty in her poem 'The Hudson Remembers', by using the river as a mirror to the attack on the Twin Towers:

> And your twin – East River –
> also remembers, as it falls with you
> into the Atlantic, where seabirds
> dive into debris like airliners

Time to shake the snow globe

I believe poets who write political poems are brave. They put their views on the written line in an attempt to make change. They are not the new romantic ameliorators who act as a palliative to privileged individuals. And I hope this essay shows that 'political' poetry can be about much more than Westminster or the White House, as it takes on all aspects of power, whether you're the proverbial landowner or tenant.

Political poets are the agents of future change. They sit alongside the tradition of artists, dramatists, novelists, as well as political commentators, in adding a voice that challenges power. Poetry should be disruptive, it should shake the snow globe of complacency, if not smash it up altogether.

Works cited:

Honest Engine – Kyle Dargan (University of Georgia Press, 2015).

Assembly Lines – Jane Commane (Bloodaxe, 2018).

Skies – Alison Brackenbury (Carcanet, 2016).

The Art of Falling – Kim Moore (Seren, 2015).

Small Hands – Mona Arshi (Pavilion Poetry, 2015).

The Fire Station – Sarah Barnsley (TellTale Press, 2015).

Dystopia 38.10 – Matt Duggan (erbacce-press, 2015).

Pepper Seed – Malika Booker (Peepal Press, 2013).

'Waiting for Boris'– Kevin *Higgins,* (source: Culture Matters, 2019).

Remember – Joy Harjo (Strawberry Press, 1981).

Scar – Carrie Etter (Shearsman Books, 2016).

Ruses and Fuses - Fran Lock (Culture Matters, 2018).

Through Your Blood Toby Campion (Burning Eye Books, 2018).

'The Hudson Remembers' – Pascale Petit (source: https://www.poetryarchive.org/poet/pascale-petit)

The Mother of Lies?
On Poetry, Fiction and Truth

Gregory Leadbetter

"I do not know what 'poetical' is: is it honest in deed and word? Is it a true thing?"– William Shakespeare, *As You Like It*

The telling connection between 'craft' and 'crafty' in English signals how deeply the mercurial relationship between cunning, ingenuity, artfulness and truth is embedded in the language, and remains perennially contentious. The question of whether poetry is "honest" and "a true thing" was central to a book that Shakespeare must have known and read. Indeed, Sir Philip Sidney's *Apologie for Poetrie* of 1595 – which remains one of the liveliest works of its kind – tackles the matter head on: the second of the four "objections to poetry" that Sidney addresses is that poetry is "the mother of lies". Sidney replies that, on the contrary, "of all writers under the sun the poet is the least liar": "to lie is to affirm that to be true which is false", whereas the poet "nothing affirms, and therefore never lieth". This may seem slippery, but the point is important: the poet is not affirming a factual truth. "The poet never maketh any circles about your imagination, to conjure you to believe for true what he writes", Sidney continues, drawing an analogy with a magus; the poet "conjures" you to do something else: the fiction of poetry acts as "an imaginative ground-plot of a profitable invention".

That phrase "profitable invention" is the key to Sidney's argument: the fact of its fictiveness – that is, its "invention" – is the very quality that makes poetry so valuable. Poetry for Sidney both encourages and relies upon "pleasure in the exercises of the mind", and educates its readers not through dogma or truth-claims, but imaginative delight, however dark the subject matter may be (remember the Elizabethan love of tragedy). It is this essentially fictive quality, says Sidney, which makes poetry a "heart-ravishing knowledge".

While I haven't noticed the revival of the kind of argument that Sidney answered, I have noticed in some quarters of contemporary poetry a kind of bafflement in the face of poems that employ, as it were, the fact of fiction. Indeed, even among practising poets, I've come across the assumption – which many of us thought long dead – that the 'I' of a poem should be read unequivocally as that of the author, which would, for example, consign the dramatic monologue to a kind of limbo. This smacks of a troubling literalism in reading and composing poetry, and the imposition of a reductive view of 'honesty' as a criterion of judgement to the detriment of what poetry can be.

Poems are often praised as 'honest', and with the best of intentions – but honesty and sincerity alone are not enough to make a poem. Where this is forgotten, poetry can all too easily slide into narcissism, where the more 'honest' a poet wishes to be (or appear), the more tired and clichéd the result. To put this another way, the poet *in effect* seeks sympathy and applause for their honesty or sincerity – for themselves – rather than the poem, or even what is ostensibly their subject.[42] The clichés of 'honesty' and 'sincerity' actually exhaust the possibility of honesty and sincerity.[43] Moreover, the practice of judging poetry according to this limited performance of honesty risks desensitising both poets and audiences not only to subtlety and nuance in language, but also to the pleasures and virtues of fiction.

Unchecked, that desensitisation can lead to impatience with anything that is not already familiar, and a limited capacity to respond to experience with curiosity, empathy and imagination. In *Through the Looking-Glass*, Alice complains

---

42   This is what makes almost every *bad* poetry reading I go to *bad*.
43   In this, I agree with Ezra Pound that *technique* is the test of a poet's sincerity.

to the Queen that "one *can't* believe impossible things". "I daresay you haven't had much practice," the Queen replies: "When I was younger, I always did it for half an hour a day. Why, sometimes I've believed as many as six impossible things before breakfast."[44] The Queen's response makes for a happy riposte to the demand for 'honesty' that I've been talking about, which ultimately tends towards the puritanical, anti-imaginative and anti-poetic. Sidney's *Apologie for Poetrie* was itself a reply to the puritanical attack on poetry by Stephen Gosson, *The Schoole of Abuse: Containing a Pleasant Invective against Poets, Pipers, Players, Jesters, and such like* (1579).[45] Instead of the joyless moralism of a Gosson, how much better to have a readerly equivalent of what Keats called 'Negative Capability', where a reader is "capable of being in uncertainties, Mysteries, doubts, without any irritable reaching after fact & reason." Of course, it's easy to understand why, when the claims of the 'real' seem so urgent, the fictive – the made-up and imaginary – can *seem* irrelevant or disconnected from life. But this is to miss the fundamental role of the fictive in our thinking and feeling – and in fact, short-circuits our grasp of reality.

A reluctance to read poetry as an essentially fictive art is related to two tendencies that, while apparently opposite in character, derive from a common root. On the one hand, there is a deeply ingrained anti-intellectual inertia, which manifests in the desire to arrive without having travelled.[46] In a letter of 1989, Ted Hughes half-jokingly summed up this attitude as: "what I don't know must be trying to oppress me". On the other hand, there is the kind of pseudo-academicism that still dominates the ways in which most people encounter poetry: this, as IA Richards put it, involves "the substitution of an intellectual

---

44   The Queen sounds like Jorge Luis Borges here. The social, political and ethical importance of *practising* belief in impossible things, as well as its liberating psychological and spiritual potential, can hardly be overstated.
45   It's telling that humour, dance and play are grouped with fiction in this 'pleasant invective': the puritanical mind (religious or not, of any place or era) sees no use in it – only mischief.
46   See the point about impatience above.

formula for a work of art".[47] Both of these attitudes tend, in practice, to reduce the poem to a paraphrasable statement of its conceptual, anecdotal or semantic content – which of course, then begs the question: why bother making (or calling) the work a 'poem' at all?

In a typically wise editorial for *The Poetry Review* in 2015, Maurice Riordan wrote of how neither a basis in 'fact', nor the kind of 'honesty' and 'sincerity' that I've been questioning here, are in themselves measures of the success of a poem:

> No doubt many poems have their source in lived experience and as such are autobiographical. But that connection should be understood as umbilical. A poem is nourished by the emotional experience of the poet but, in so far as it succeeds, it is freed from the circumstance and contingency of the life. Even so-called confessional poetry, when it is poetry, enters the autonomous realm of fiction, where we can access it as readers without asking if it's true.[48]

Calling reality into being

There are and can be many kinds of poem, and the last thing I would want to do is (as Coleridge once put it) "introduce an act of Uniformity against Poets". Rather, my purpose in this essay is to draw attention to, and to make a case for an attitude and a perspective towards the fictive – both in the poet and the reader – at risk of being marginalised.

Of course, there are countless examples of the fictive in poetry –

---

47   As Dana Gioia puts it in his excellent essay 'Poetry as Enchantment': "critics, scholars, and teachers need to recognize and respect non-conceptual forms of knowledge, which are fundamental to all forms of literature, especially poetry . . . We need to create and cultivate in our classrooms a dialectic of intellect and intuition, of mental attention and sensory engagement."

48   Sarah Howe's *Loop of Jade*, which, among its many other techniques, uses an imaginary book from Borges – practically the patron saint of fiction – as a structural principle, springs to mind as a perfect example of what Riordan describes.

and quite a few playful defences of its 'lies'. Touchstone's reply to Audrey's question – this essay's epigraph – is a famous one: "the truest poetry is the most feigning". Auden used this phrase as the title for a comic poem (with the subtitle 'Ars Poetica for Hard Times') in which the speaker exhorts the reader to "Be subtle, various, ornamental, clever", and performs what he suggests while mocking humankind:

> With no more nature in his loving smile
> Than in his theories of a natural style,
> What but tall tales, the luck of verbal playing,
> Can trick his lying nature into saying
> That love, or truth in any serious sense,
> Like orthodoxy, is a reticence?

What but the trick of a fiction might draw a reticent truth from a "lying nature"'? There's a neat conundrum, which might have appealed to a poet steeped in such paradox: Michael Donaghy. His poem 'Smith' plays on the tension between truth, performance and fiction in its focus on the forging of identity and the writing of a signature:

> Why does it seem to take a forger's nerve
> To make my signature come naturally?
> Naturally? But every signature's
> A trick we learn to do, consistently,
> Like Queequeg's cross, or Whistler's butterfly.

The entire poem, like 'Erratum', 'The Excuse', and so many others of his, opens up with performative verve and knowing concision the living connection between authenticity and affectation – or, to put it another way, between truth and artfulness.[49] To grasp the resonance of what's in play in that

---

49   Don Paterson's commentary on Donaghy's work, *Smith: A Reader's Guide to the Poetry of Michael Donaghy*, brings these themes out nicely: 'An artist's allegiance is to the truth, not the facts, and facts are often the things you have to change to make the poem more truthful'. Donaghy isn't alone in exploring such connections, of course: see for example Jon Stone's *School of Forgery*, which takes fabrication (in both senses of the word) as its subject.

connection, it helps to go back once again to past controversies that (to adapt William Faulkner) aren't even past.

In the *Apologie for Poetrie*, Sidney describes poetry as "a representing, counterfeiting, or figuring forth", and writes that the poet, "with the vigour of his own invention, doth grow in effect another nature, in making things either better than Nature bringeth forth, or, quite anew, forms such as never were in Nature . . . so as he goeth hand in hand with Nature, not enclosed within the narrow warrant of her gifts, but freely ranging only within the zodiac of his own wit." For Sidney the figurative language of poetry generates a "second nature", a reality that – spun from the "zodiac" of his creative intelligence – exists, but which cannot be found in the forms of nature.

Nearly a century later, the philosopher John Locke was having none of it. In *An Essay Concerning Human Understanding*, he wrote that, "all the figurative application of Words, Eloquence hath invented, are for nothing else but to insinuate wrong ideas, move the Passions, and thereby mislead the Judgement." The ideal that (with the best of intentions) Locke implicitly sets against the poetic use of language is that of 'plain speaking' – the promise of an *unmediated* truth – and here we are back to the kind of argument (often inspired by puritanical religion) that Sidney was countering in the *Apologie*. But is it even possible to attain to an *unmediated* truth, given that every aspect of our experience – our nervous system, our physiology, our habitat, and of course our language – involves a *medium*?

A century and more after Locke, the poets and thinkers we now call the Romantics took up the problem, and – especially in Coleridge – it is Sidney's ideas of poetry and the poet that find new life. Coleridge recognised that Locke's rejection of figurative language also, in effect, rejects the imagination, and hence the authority of imaginative literature in and over our experience. For Coleridge, the life of language is inherently figurative, not least because it involves *connotation* as well as *denotation*: words *imply* and *suggest* more than their dictionary meaning. Even the word 'literal' – used as the opposite of 'figurative' – is (look, John Locke!) figurative. Coleridge's writing and thinking on poetry attempted to describe how the power of language not only represents reality – it constitutes and calls reality into being. "It is among the miseries of the present age," Coleridge wrote, "that it recognises no medium between *Literal* and *Metaphorical*."

Coleridge wrote that in his poetry of the supernatural – as in 'The Rime of the Ancient Mariner' and 'Christabel' – he attempted to procure in the reader 'that willing suspension of disbelief for the moment, which constitutes poetic faith', and in this lies the crux of his poetics. Seduced by the poem into a state of active fascination, in which they imagine more than they *know*, the spiritual, intellectual and emotional life of the reader is aroused and the aperture of their being dilates to allow the ingress of a new, expanded reality.[50] Such faith in the productive power of language speaks in stark contrast to the arguments in Gosson and Locke. On this view, poetry is a form of invocation in which artfulness generates the in-the-moment truth of the reader's experience.[51]

Coleridge saw that poetry also moves beyond the literal in the intensity of its attention to 'the excitement of vision by sound and the exponents of sound'. In this he anticipated later interest in the auricular form of poetry, such as Amy Lowell's 'Poetry as a Spoken Art', which emphasised 'the essential kinship of poetry and music', and Velimir Khlebnikov's writings on 'beyonsense': the magical 'double life' of words as both physiologically affective sound and semantic, conceptual sense. These writers recognise that the affective power of language operates upon us both before and after the 'literal', denotative sense of the words, and that this power, in touching

---

50   In this state of mind, Coleridge said, 'our common notions of philosophy give way'.

51   It is no coincidence that, etymologically, the word 'romantic' means 'story-like': the 'romantic' is rooted in the fictive resources of our being.

the sub- and supra-verbal life of our bodies, finds its way past the merely rational understanding: hence it is, as Eliot wrote, that 'genuine poetry can communicate before it is understood'.

So then: what is "poetical"? Is it "honest" in deed and word? Is it a "true" thing? As Sidney points out, the word "poet" means "maker" (which, he notes, was, "whether by luck or wisdom", a common word for "poet" among the English) and – in the perspective and attitude towards poetry that I've emphasised here – the poet can be read as a maker of truth, in and through the action of his fiction.

Poetry *is* the manipulation of experience, and the generation of experience: hence Yeats writes that the purpose of rhythm is to prolong the moment of contemplation. Poetry has designs on our very being. As Robert Lowell put it (following both Coleridge and Wallace Stevens), "Poetry is not the record of an event: it is an event." To rework Lowell a little: a poem embodies and invokes a psychic event. It is in this sense that, as Colin Falck contends in his book *Myth, Truth and Literature*, "Fictions reveal reality". In poetry, the end is in the means.

In English, at least, art will never escape the double-edged sense that 'artful' conveys, but it is no bad thing to have such doubleness so deeply implicated in the medium in which the poet must work. No language can escape the effects of artfulness – or its absence. It is through its artfulness – its fictive qualities – that, in RP Blackmur's words, poetry "adds to the stock of available reality".

This is My Truth, Tell Me Yours: On Writing the Real

Jane Commane

"Now I think poetry will save nothing from oblivion, but I keep writing about the ordinary because for me it's the home of the extraordinary, the only home."
— Philip Levine

Postcards from the Edge(lands)

The world you'll find in my first collection of poems, *Assembly Lines*, is based in the Midlands landscapes I grew up in and the people I grew up alongside; a real but also an imagined place. It exists within me as well as outside and all around me. When Roy Fisher writes "Birmingham is what I think with", I know entirely what he means, even if for me, it's a sort of 'greater Midlands' I think with.

My family spent most of their lifetimes working in Coventry's factories, the names of which echoed through childhood like an imposing cast of steely gentry – GEC, Alvis, Rover. This was the 1980s and early 1990s, a politicised time, charged with a uniquely Midlands sensibility of being and belonging that relied on a deeply uneasy sense of not really belonging and feeling deeply uncomfortable about the idea of being. Later, those industrial names came to mean something else – vast sites of derelict brick and concrete, where megalithic distribution parks would, by the turn of the millennium, dominate for miles around.

I was surrounded by people who were extraordinary storytellers, and I was a voracious reader. But our lives and realities were not often the kind I found in literature; instead, in my teens I found echoes of reality in the lyrics of the bands I loved. The lightning bolt that earthed my own awakening of place and self, and my desire to write poetry, was a second-hand copy of the Bloodaxe anthology, *The New Poetry*. Here, the electricity leapt between some of the music I'd been listening to and the poems I read. Another world opened that was actively political (Ian McMillan's 'Pit Closure as Art'), weirdly beautiful (Selima Hill's 'Monkeys'), satirical or caustically searing (Peter Reading's 'Evagatory'). I didn't understand all of it, but I was intrigued and excited by it. These poems felt like secret and radical knowledge.

In 2001, I picked up a novel called *From Blue to Black* by Joel Lane in my local library. Knowing nothing of the author I was attracted because, not only was it about music, but it was set in Birmingham. I hadn't yet realised you could (or were allowed to) write about the Midlands, yet here it was, in Lane's sharp, brutal prose – the city and all its nightlife and music and grimy giddy rush. The excitement of recognition aside, reading this distinctly Midlands Noir was deeply significant. Maybe I didn't have to be somewhere exciting to write – maybe somewhere exciting was right here and now in my own small-town reality, especially if no one else was writing it.

The spirit level

For me, writing poetry from real life is an act of love and memory, of documentation and celebration: writing back into literature the lives of those I know and love, making sure that the thousand hours of twilight shifts and safety boots aren't lost by being untold. But that balance of documentation and celebration is vital – both elements in equilibrium – one keeping the other in a constant check to ensure I neither tell things too matter-of-factly, nor allow myself to slip into sentimental, romanticised versions of reality. This is my poetry spirit level.

When I write poetry that begins in real life, I'm not aiming towards creating an unquestionable, unshifting edifice that regards itself as The Truth. But rather I write towards something more modest – to be honest with myself, to render real life and people truthfully and do them justice, but to also find routes into reality that are playful, imaginative, serious; to write towards a truth drawn from life which I hope readers find open to them.

I aim to write towards something accurate from experience which others might find a truth for themselves within. But also I am keen to avoid that limiting and fraught territory whereby a poet assumes an authorial mantle of Truth or Reality, and risks being didactic. This can raise all kinds of questions: whose truth are you telling, and who gives you permission to do so? Are you doing justice to those experiences and those lives? Are you at risk of proclaiming the truth from on high? Who is this for? Is this real, but not especially truthful or honest? Is there room in the poem for your readers, room for imagination, room for doubt, room for more than one thing at once, or what Keats termed 'negative capability'?

What a good poem achieves in keeping its levels balanced is that it dares to be accurate but not to be closed off; it leaves room for the reader to enter its space and enable some form of realisation or shift of perspective– however elemental or tiny – within its confines.

In a thought-provoking essay on poetry, truth and protest, Rachel Tzvia Back describes her own spirit level – a "poetic holy trinity" – as: "(1) the drive toward accuracy and truth-telling; (2) the personal accountability of the poetic, and (3) the magic of intertwined meaning and music.", then proceeds to expand on that first point: that "Poetry as a language art exists on its accuracy; less than accurate is unacceptable to the poet." In terms of that fine balance between reality and imaginations, Back notes that:

> I do believe that in the interface between what Wallace
> Stevens termed "the pressure of reality" and the wonders
> of imagination and talent—in the ongoing interplay

between the personal and the political—the true poet, being truthful, may offer us alternative versions of and even redemptive visions for our troubled world.[52]

If our poems work towards this point of accuracy, it presents us not with limits but rather with freedom; the chance to imagine other realities and possibilities. And, to borrow a few words from Jane Austen, to write towards those greater truths that can be "universally acknowledged". In sharing and writing into experience ambitiously, accurately, open to a spectrum of imaginative options, we emerge towards a point of commonality through the imaginative space, where everything is possible. As poet and priest Mark Oakley has it, "Poetry doesn't have a single view in mind; it has multiple meanings on the go. Here, truth is rich in connectivity. It is riotously vivid."[53]

The poetic oven gloves: techniques for writing the real

Having thrown all of this at you, you may be wondering how the poet should begin to approach the idea of reality, real life and the various modes of 'true life' and 'truth' in writing their own poems. And for a moment, let's remind ourselves that *every* writer will innately draw upon their own realities; whether we like it or not, our lives, experiences and knowledge fall into our writing just as our shadow casts over the page we write on.

There may also be times when that closeness to reality will bring additional considerations and difficulties to our poems. Sometimes, these may be deeply personal truths – our backstory may include things that are hard to write, whether these are traumatic or even simply things unsaid. There may also be occasions when writers must balance truthfulness in their writing with the wish to avoid unnecessary hurt to others.

---

52   https://www.worldliteraturetoday.org/2014/may/species-magic-role-poetry-protest-and-truth-telling-israeli-poets-perspective

53   The splash of words: believing in poetry – https://www.youtube.com/watch?v=VNuzbhABwTo

Some real experiences and truths may be too hot to handle; some might even be toxic, flammable, harmful and require us to don goggles and make sure we've read the risk assessment first. We may need to grab our oven gloves so we can heave these bubbling, troubling pots from the stove and serve them up safely. In these instances, it is poetic device and technique (the oven gloves of my metaphor) that will allow us to both be truthful and get close, but also to approach those truths and realities safely and handle them with care.

We should consider too that there is always room in our poems for the ordinary and everyday experiences that can be just as transformative and revelatory, as well as space for our imagination – for invention, absurdity and fiction as a path towards truth. If something true and revealing comes via a fictional or technical device within the poem, it is no less revelatory than if it comes to us via a moment of direct honesty or self-revelation. For instance, I have no idea whether the events described in Paul Durcan's poem 'Golden Mothers Driving West' (a truly extraordinary poem, seek it out) ever happened wholly or partially in real life – but the extraordinary *truth* it leaves the reader with is almost devastating.

Here are three techniques you can apply to your own poems, whether the realities they deal with are ordinary or extraordinary:

It's the way you tell 'em

Poems based in real-life stories can risk simply being anecdote retold in poem form; the writer caught between exploring the truth at the heart of the situation and needing to be an exacting, truthful narrator. "But that's how it happened," they say, as you offer critique on the twenty-stanza poem about an ancestor's thwarted first love, "It's all true, she really was a milkmaid in Fife."

Be prepared to not only leave some of the details of a true story on the cutting-room floor, but to find a way to circle in on an idea, rather than simply pounce on it and tell the linear narrative. Could that story be better told through a dream, a fragment, a voicemail from the past? Could it be told by accident, overhead in gossip? Perhaps, in pouring milk into a cup of tea, the story of Great Aunt Ailsa from Glenrothes, and all that unrequited love, could be allowed to pour out in a way we didn't quite expect.

Make it strange

I'm currently writing a sequence of poems about my encounters with social class. What I'm keen to avoid in these is relaying the anecdote of a situation, and in first draft form, the poems seemed flat and didactic. So I began to re-write each differently. A job interview in which class privilege came into play was put through the filter of the absurd and became, instead, a job interview with sea-lions. Diverting into the animal world afforded me creative freedom, allowing me to take the heat off the human reality, to be funny, to be more exact and truthful than I could have been with those real people in mind. It was only by going to those extremes and various ridiculousnesses that the reality of class, itself in so many ways extreme and ridiculous, could be explored in a way that didn't feel heavy-handed.

This is a process of defamiliarisation, and by making the familiar and known absurd or weird, we are not taken further from the truth but, counterintuitively, allowed to get closer to it. The parallels that our imagination creates holds a crazed and fractured mirror to allow us to see our realities and truths in all their facets; a whole hall of mirrors in which the real aspects we try to ignore are presented back to us exaggerated, distorted, all the more unavoidable.

If the reality you're writing towards feels too obvious or anecdotal, why not try to see it again in a new or strange scenario rather than a common one? Change one crucial thing about the real life experience. Use humour, defamiliarisation or deflection in your poems. If it doesn't work with a human saying it, play at throwing your voice. Within this strange play, allow what is most true to come across without binding everything in the poem in an absolute marriage with reality.

Forms of truth

In writing towards a reality or a truth, poetic form – or at the very least some decision about the vessel you're about to pour this truth into – is essential. This isn't to say you must use a traditional or strict poetic form, but rather suggest that you find a way to contain and shape what you need to say and make a deliberate decision about line lengths, stanzas or layout. With the sequences I mention writing above, I adopted rules for myself about the shape I would use to form and contain the poem; loosely based on a sonnet form, but with longer lines to allow for a blockier poem, using 14 lines of 14 syllables. I call this a 'fourteener'.

The more complex, emotive or personal the subject, the more useful it can be to implement a form. This decision can be made post first-draft – it may be useful to not limit or introduce a form too early if it may stop you writing openly and freely towards what you need to say in that vital first draft. Once you have a draft, you can switch into the imposition of a form or shape of your choosing to refine and reform the poem. However, as with my funny little 14x14 poems, some poems come about precisely because the form makes you do something particular or peculiar from the very first step in order to release something.

Form, along with these other techniques, can make certain demands of you, preoccupying the conscious, meddling mind and freeing the deeper unconscious imagination. This in turn allows for more surprising elements, ideas and modes of approach to rise to the surface, and will help you, without realising, to find your way closer to your own truth or reality. Whether this is ordinary, extraordinary or in-between – technique and the process of play and experimentation of poetry helps you to find a way to say, at last, all the things you never realised you really wanted to say.

CODA

34 Interrogations: The Questions You Should Ask Yourself When Writing a Poem

Roger Robinson

1. Is the poem efficient?
2. Does the poem have any risk in it?
3. Does the title of the poem entice the reader into reading it, whilst casting a shadow of meaning on the poem?
4. Does every line of the poem beg you as the writer to stay?
5. Are you reviving an uncommonly used form?
6. When you were moving from your first draft into your form, what were your organising principles?
7. Does the poem contain specific music, imagery, imagination, story, and structure?
8. Is there too much of one and not enough of the others?
9. Does the music of the poem reflect or reject the subtext and or subject of the poem?
10. Does the imagery of the poem reflect or reject the subtext and or subject of the poem?
11. Have you read and analysed at least two good poetry collections before attempting to write this poem?
12. Has someone written a similar poem that's much better than your attempt?
13. Do you have a firm hold on the formal history of the form you're trying to write in and its modern variants?
14. Does the poem have moments of heightened or striking language?

15. Are you reviving any old and or uncommon words?

16. Have you read the poem aloud? Have you had someone else read it aloud?

17. Have you used any cinematic narrative techniques in the poem?

18. Does the poem tip its hat to tradition whilst keeping a keen eye on innovation?

19. Are you showing us a new way to see something in the poem?

20. Does the central idea unfold as the poem goes on?

21. Can the poem stand alone?

22. Is the poem a part of a series?

23. Do the arguments in your poem teach your reader anything about their life?

24. Does the poem make you uncomfortable?

25. Does the poem make the reader uncomfortable? Is that good? Is it better that than the poem being boring?

26. Are you bored? Is the poem boring?

27. Can the poem be simplified without becoming simplistic?

28. Is the poem about people's lives, or about you and your big head?

29. Are you the hero of this poem? Of all your poems?

30. Does the poem push at the boundaries of your taste?

31. Are you writing the same poem again and again?

32. Is your poem allergic to all current literary trends?

33. Can you add no more to the poem? Can you take nothing else out?

34. What's the poem you least want to write? Why aren't you writing that poem?

Giving Off Sparks: Writing Prompts

Moniza Alvi – Bird-and-human-watching

Watch a bird (or birds) attentively for about 10 minutes, or longer. Try to describe its activity as precisely as you can, the way it flies, lands, rests, takes off, hops out of a bush, takes a bath, for instance. How does it make you feel? Does it remind you of anything? Consider the setting, record the sounds, colours, smells...

When you note these ideas down as possible lines of a poem, experiment with making the words move on the page by indenting or scattering them. You can create cadence, darting motion and surprise, perhaps inspired by Sujata Bhatt's use of line-breaks and the layout in her poem 'The Peacock'. You might use the second person 'you' as she does, and watch yourself, watching the bird. Think of your poem-in-the-making as a musical score.

Dean Atta – Persona poetry

- Pick a fairytale character, mythological figure, superhero or a celebrity that you find interesting.
- Think of how this character relates to you? How are they similar or different to you?
- In the persona of this character, free write for five minutes on each of the following:

    1. My greatest dream is ...
    2. My greatest fear is ...
    3. My favourite place is ...
    4. My favourite song is ...

A free write is when you write without stopping or editing. The aim is to write for the whole of the allotted time without pause for thought. You are generating raw material. At this stage, use preexisting knowledge and your imagination rather than looking anything up. You can fact-check and research after your free write.

- Use raw material from your free write and any research to write the persona poem. Keep in mind any similarities or differences you have to this character and how this may create a subtext within the poem.
- Begin your poem, "They call me ..." e.g. "They call me The Little Mermaid."

Liz Berry – A small glinting treasure

Dig up a small glinting treasure from your word hoard. It might be a dialect word, slang or a made-up family word. Now write a love letter to it. Tell the word why you love it and how it makes you feel to hear it or say it. Think of the shape and sound of the word, all that it suggests to you and conjures up.

Dear tranklements, dear hinny, dear blooth...

Debjani Chatterjee – A ghazal finale

Write a *maqtaa* – a ghazal's final *sher* or couplet. It should be able to stand alone, without the need to be preceded by any other *sher*. Like every *sher*, it must have a r*adif* or refrain at the end of the second line, and a *qaafiyaa* or rhyming word just before the *radif*. Also include a *takhallus,* or pen name, somewhere. If the *maqtaa* is for a ghazal adaptation, you can insert any character's name.

Carrie Etter – Infused with feeling

Think about how you're feeling at this very moment – honestly! Are you feeling tired, happy, angry, frustrated, lustful, hopeful, pensive? Now look around the room you find yourself in, or if the weather allows, go outside. What would it be like if this place were infused with your feeling? What if the otherwise innocent looking painting on the wall suddenly became menacing or sorrowful or whatever it is you've been feeling? And what about that chair, that tree, the cat? Allow for 3-5 sentences of feeling-infused description, then conclude with a declaration, something that follows from these feelings but feels like a large jump forward from it. For example, Angela Veronica Wang's poem about the atmosphere on driving into 'Louisiana' ends "Louisiana was always close to God" and Jefferson Navicky's speaker in 'Teeth' looks across a lake to Canada and concludes, "I tasted everything that was North." This final sentence may take a few tries to get right, but making such a cognitive leap successfully will make for a powerful conclusion. Good luck!

Will Harris – The comparandum

Put your thumbs over your eyes and empty out your mind. Let stress, if there is stress, pass through you like a sheet of overcooked lasagna floating in the enormity of deep space. Imagine yourself as wood or brass suddenly become an instrument, the form emanating from you, each thought hatching (*l'éclosion*) and stumbling into the light. Free-write a page of notes. Imagine yourself as filling up a beaker rather than writing a page. Read Sappho 105a. Write the second half of a simile without knowing the comparandum, then imagine alternative comparandums; e.g. "like a biscuit soaked in the moon-flavoured sweat of two elephants." The comparandum: "tiramisu? walking through Lampton at 5 in the morning? the love of distant cousins?"

Tania Hershman – Change of perspective

Take a poem-in-progress and change the point of view: if it was 'I' make it 'you', if it was 'you' make it 'we', if it was 'he' or 'she' try 'I'. Read it out to yourself. What difference does this shift make to the story your poem is telling? Try this again with another point of view, see how it feels when you read it to yourself. Keep doing this until the poem feels like it's closest to the one you want to write. If none of the points of view quite feel right, try moving from one to another within the poem. Mix it up. Let yourself slip out of your comfort zone and see what happens.

Peter Kahn – Mine for striking lines

Each day mine for striking lines from the newspaper, a book you're reading and/or a song you're listening to. Use one to create a new golden shovel poem.

Gregory Leadbetter – Ghost of a mountain

This is an entry from one of Coleridge's notebooks:

> 'Poems. — Ghost of a mountain / the forms seizing my body, as I passed, became realities — I, a Ghost, till I had reconquered my Substance /.'

Write that poem, or poems.

Harry Man – Make a link that does not yet exist

A few years ago I was working on a story featuring Julius Caesar, Marie Curie, Billy the Kid and Helen of Troy. They are all having this wild conversation about – if they could have their time again – where in the world they might go to receive the best education. Of course, it turns out we're at a fancy dress party and our first person protagonist feels that at any minute, he'll lose his grip on reality, while he gradually works his way through the wrapper of a small Italian chocolate. Later that night we end up in the hard, cold glitter of the rain, talking to the ghost of his wife who is surrounded by a halo of golden light, telling him that there's nothing he can do now about having the wrong kind of insurance.

For this prompt, do the same thing in your poem and make a link that does not yet exist between two adverts. These can be adverts you've seen online, or something you've seen elsewhere. What's the story that connects the two? If you prefer not to use an advert, you can choose a pair of lines from Pentametron – a wonderful little online bot that selects lines of iambic pentameter from Twitter and retweets them. You can scroll through its tweets and select your own here: https://twitter.com/pentametron/. If you're interested in going down the afterlife route, you can also have a look at the upbeat and sweet poem that hid behind the story, *Zimmer Imagines Heaven* by Paul Zimmer and use it for inspiration.

Roy McFarlane – Writing into the unknown

Find a blank sheet of A4 paper: fold it down the middle and rip or cut it in half. You should now have two A5 pieces of paper. Put one aside and take the other piece of A5 paper and repeat the above. You should now have two A6 pieces.

Think of an historical event, something that means a lot to you personally, something you wanted to research, or something that had a major impact on yourself or your family. I want you to google or scour through newspapers or reports and write down a line that encapsulates the event. Begin writing in the constraints of the A6 piece of paper and stop writing when you've filled the space. Remember, whether it's two lines with breaks or ten lines compressed, that's okay.

Writing into confined and limited spaces affects the way you write; the lines might be shorter. A long line might force you to break the line and indent it on the second line. Play with these pieces of paper, portrait or landscape.

Now, look for another line or maybe a song, or sporting event, or a film that was playing during that period and begin writing on the second A6 piece of paper. Again, keep writing until you've filled the space.

Finally, write your own personal story of what you were doing during this eventful time. If you weren't born during that period, create a character, be imaginative, inhabit an individual of that period.

You should have three pieces of paper, of various sizes. Patterns may form, line lengths may differ, line breaks in unusual places. You may have a narrative developing or they might be three separate conversations. Place them side by side and see what happens.

Clare Pollard – Homophonic translation

Homophonic translation is a fun exercise that really makes us think about how we might carry sounds across from one text to another. In the 1960s, Celia and Louis Zukofsky translated Catullus, trying to make a text out of English words that sounded very similar. So this:

CATULLUS 70
Nulli se dicit mulier mea nubere malle
quam mihi, non si se Iuppiter ipse petat.
dicit: sed mulier cupido quod dicit amanti,
in vento et rapida scribere oportet aqua.

Became this:

Newly say dickered my love air my own would marry me all
whom but me, none see say Jupiter if she petted.
Dickered: said my love air could be o could dickered a man too
in wind o wet rapid a scribble reported in water.

Pick a poem in a language you don't know and concentrate on mimicking the sounds in English. It's a great way of homing in on whether a poet uses techniques like assonance or alliteration, and also testing whether Frost's concept of the 'sound of sense' works in reality!

Peter Raynard – Political power

Write from a position of power and all its delusion. Explain how wonderful everything is, and how grateful people should be, *or* still write from a position of power, but one of contrition, resignation (i.e. something you wouldn't normally hear from a person in power).

Jacqueline Saphra – Sonnet address

Write a sonnet addressed to someone close to you in iambic pentameter bearing in mind the argument in the octet (first eight lines) and the counterargument in the sestet (final six lines). Use the following rhyming words at the end of each line:

> much, self, shelf, touch, lunch, stealth, health, judge, find, hoarse, youth, kind, doors, truth.

Joelle Taylor – Six scenes

Take a sheet of A4 white paper and divide it into six boxes, so that they make a story board or cartoon strip.

You now have six boxes to tell your life story. Remember that poetry is cinema so use your pen as a camera and guide the reader into your scenes. What six images would you use? Would you have an extended metaphor that can contain each scene (a boxing ring, for example)? Write as visually and as concisely as you can; each verse must be contained in an individual box.

Marvin Thompson – Sestina in seven seconds

Write a sestina about the last 7 seconds in the life of a stag beetle. Each stanza could be headed with a countdown: 7 ... 6 ... 5 ...

Don't like beetles? How about the last 7 days in the life of the first woman on Mars / Margaret Thatcher / Lazarus...?

Julia Webb – A memory mining exercise

This is a good way to free you up and get memories flowing. Start each line with "I remember" and just keep going – thoughts that come up can be from any time in your life and don't have to be related to one another.

In the second part of the exercise take one of the memories and expand on it – don't be precious about the actual details – it is okay to change things if it makes the poem better. You might have to have two or three attempts at writing about the same subject before you get one you are happy with. Try using the titles or formal names of people you are writing about rather than their names - for example: my mother, your mother, father, brother, uncle, Mr Smith etc.

Antosh Wojcik – Happenings

Find five blank pieces of paper, set them out in front of you. Head four of them with these four titles:

1. 'something that happened'
2. 'something that didn't happen'
3. 'something that happened today'
4. 'something that will happen'

Fill out these pieces, documenting events that correspond with the titles. Try to keep the writing limited to the recording of events. Titles 2 & 4 should be fictional.

Title the last blank piece of paper 'Phone Call' (this is your working title).

Now, correlate all four events into one poem and write them in the tone of your voice on the phone. Feel free to arrange the events in any order and distort them, but you must include all four.

FURTHER READING

The best recommendation to improve your poetry writing is always to read more poems and poets – especially those from countries, traditions and aesthetics different from your own.

In addition, below are some books that I turn to when my writing needs a lift, a change of direction, a re-charge; or there's a pressing need to answer a more technical question, or consider something from a different angle. – *RD*

'How to' guides

52: Write a poem a week. Start Now. Keep Going – Jo Bell and guest poets (Nine Arches Press, 2015).

How to be a Poet: A 21ˢᵗ Century Guide to Writing Well – Jo Bell and Jane Commane (Nine Arches Press, 2017).

The Ode Less Travelled: Unlocking the Poet Within – Stephen Fry (Arrow, 2007).

An Introduction to English Poetry – James Fenton (Penguin, 2003).

Cambridge Introduction to Creative Writing – David Morley (Cambridge Introductions to Literature, 2011).

The Practice of Poetry: Writing Exercises From Poets Who Teach – edited by Robin Behn and Chase Twichell (William Morrow Paperbacks, 1992).

Writing Poems – Peter Sansom (Bloodaxe, 1993).

Writing Poetry – W. N. Herbert (Routledge, 2009).

Essay collections

Stress Fractures: Essays on Poetry – ed. Tom Chivers (Penned in the Margins, 2010).

The Redress of Poetry – Seamus Heaney (Faber & Faber, 2002).

The Bars of Atlantis – Durs Grünbein (Farrar, Straus and Giroux, 2010).

Forgive The Language: Essays on Poets and Poetry – Katy Evans-Bush (Penned in the Margins, 2015).

Madness, Rack, and Honey: Collected Lectures – Mary Ruefle (Wave Books, 2012).

Don't Ask Me What I Mean: Poets in Their Own Words – edited by Don Paterson and Clare Brown (Picador, 2012).

In Their Own Words: Contemporary Poets on their Poetry – edited by Helen Ivory and George Szirtes (Salt Publishing, 2012).

On Poetry – Glyn Maxwell (Oberon Books, 2012 / 2017).

Poetry in the Making: A Handbook for Writing and Teaching – Ted Hughes (Faber & Faber 1967 / 2008).

Strong Words: Modern Poets on Modern Poetry – edited by W. N. Herbert and Matthew Hollis (Bloodaxe, 2000).

On Poetry – Jonathan Davidson (Smith I Doorstop, 2018).

More inspiration

#Afterhours – Inua Ellams (Nine Arches Press, 2017).

The New Penguin Book of English Verse – ed Paul Keegan (Penguin, 2000).

Faces of Love: Hafez and the Poets of Shiraz – translated by Dick Davis (Penguin Classics, 2014).

101 Sonnets – Don Paterson (Faber & Faber, 2012).

The Golden Shovel Anthology: New Poems Honoring Gwendolyn Brooks – eds. Dr Peter Kahn, Ravi Shankar, Patricia Smith (University of Arkansas Press, 2017).

The Penguin Book of the Prose Poem: From Baudelaire to Anne Carson – ed. Jeremy Noel-Tod (Penguin, 2019).

Adventures in Form A Compendium of New Poetic Forms – ed. Tom Chivers (Penned in the Margins, 2012).

CONTRIBUTORS

Moniza Alvi was born in Lahore in 1954 to a Pakistani father and an English mother. She grew up in Hertfordshire. Her poetry collections include *The Country at My Shoulder* (OUP, 1993) which was shortlisted for the Whitbread and the TS Eliot poetry prizes, *Europa* (Bloodaxe, 2008) and *At the Time of Partition* (Bloodaxe, 2013), both also shortlisted for the TS Eliot Prize. Her most recent collection is *Blackbird, Bye Bye* (Bloodaxe, 2018).

Dean Atta was named as one of the most influential LGBT people in the UK by *The Independent on Sunday*. He was shortlisted for the Polari First Book Prize for his debut poetry collection, *I Am Nobody's Nigger*. His poems have been anthologised by Bad Betty Press, Emma Press and Platypus Press. He is a member of Keats House Poets Forum and Malika's Poetry Kitchen. His novel, *The Black Flamingo*, was published in August 2019.

Liz Berry's first book of poems, *Black Country* (Chatto 2014), described as a "sooty, soaring hymn to her native West Midlands" (*The Guardian*) won the Somerset Maugham Award, the Geoffrey Faber Memorial Award and Forward Prize for Best First Collection 2014. Her pamphlet *The Republic of Motherhood* (Chatto, 2018) was a Poetry Book Society Pamphlet choice and the title poem won the Forward Prize for Best Single Poem 2018.

Caroline Bird has five collections of poetry published by Carcanet. Her most recent, *In These Days of Prohibition*, was shortlisted for the 2017 TS Eliot Prize and the Ted Hughes Award. A two-time winner of the Foyles Young Poets Award, her first collection *Looking Through Letterboxes* was published in 2002 when she was 15. She won an Eric Gregory Award in 2002, and was shortlisted for the Geoffrey Dearmer Prize in 2001 and the Dylan Thomas Prize in 2008 and 2010. She was one of the five official poets at the 2012 London Olympics. Her sixth collection, *The Air Year*, will be published in 2020.

Malika Booker is a British poet of Guyanese and Grenadian Parentage. *Breadfruit* (flippedeye, 2007) received a Poetry Book Society pamphlet recommendation and her poetry collection *Pepper Seed* (Peepal Tree Press, 2013) was longlisted for the OCM Bocas prize and shortlisted for the Seamus Heaney Centre prize. She is published with Sharon Olds and Warsan Shire in *The Penguin Modern Poet Series 3: Your Family: Your Body* (2017). She is a Fellow of The Complete Works and Cave Canem and was inaugural Poet in Residence at the Royal Shakespeare Company. Malika has an MA in Creative and Life Writing from Goldsmiths University, and is currently a poetry Lecturer at Manchester Metropolitan University

Debjani Chatterjee MBE FRSL is an Indian-born, Sheffield-based, creative arts psychotherapist and RLF Fellow, who has written, translated and edited 70 books. Described as a poet "full of wit and charm" (Andrew Motion), her eight poetry collections include *Namaskar: New & Selected Poems*. She has edited award-winning anthologies including *The Redbeck Anthology of British South Asian Poetry*. Her books for children include *The Elephant-Headed God & Other Hindu Tales* (a Children's Book of the Year). www.dchatterjeewriter. simplesite.com

Jane Commane's debut collection, *Assembly Lines*, was published by Bloodaxe in 2018, and longlisted for the 2019 Michael Murphy Memorial Prize. Her poetry has featured in *The Best British Poetry 2011* (Salt Publishing) and *The Guardian*. In 2016, she was selected for Writing West Midlands' Room 204 writer development programme, and awarded a Jerwood Compton Poetry Fellowship in 2017. Jane is editor at Nine Arches Press, and co-author (with Jo Bell) of *How to Be a Poet*.

Rishi Dastidar's poetry has been published by the *Financial Times*, BBC and Southbank Centre amongst many others. A fellow of The Complete Works, the Arts Council England funded programme for BAME poets in the UK, he is a consulting editor at *The Rialto* magazine, a member of the Malika's Poetry Kitchen collective, and chair of the writer development organization Spread The Word. His collections are *Ticker-tape* and *Saffron Jack*, both published by Nine Arches Press.

Carrie Etter is the author of four collections of poetry, a chapbook of flash fictions, and numerous essays and reviews. Her prose poems have appeared in *The Penguin Book of the Prose Poem, Iowa Review, PN Review, Poetry Review, Westerly,* and many other periodicals and anthologies. She is Reader in Creative Writing at Bath Spa University.

Will Harris is a poet and critic from London. He is the author of the chapbook, *All This Is Implied,* and the essay *Mixed-Race Superman,* published by Peninsula Press in the UK and Melville House in the US. His poems have appeared in *The Guardian, The London Review of Books,* and the anthology *Ten: Poets of the New Generation.* His debut poetry collection, *RENDANG,* is forthcoming from Granta in February 2020.

Tania Hershman is the author of a poetry collection, *Terms and Conditions* (Nine Arches, 2017), three short story collections, and a poetry pamphlet. Her second pamphlet, joint winner of the 2019 Live Canon Poetry Pamphlet competition, will be published in November 2019, and a hybrid poetry/prose pamphlet is forthcoming from Guillemot Press in March 2020. Tania has a PhD in creative writing inspired by particle physics, is curator of ShortStops and co-founder of OnThisDayShe. www.taniahershman.com.

A high school teacher based in Chicago, **Peter Kahn** runs the largest school-based Spoken Word Club in the world. He has twice been a commended poet in the Poetry Society's National Poetry Competition. He co-founded the London Teenage Poetry Slam and, as a Visiting Fellow at Goldsmiths, founded the Spoken Word Education Training Programme. A founding member of Malika's Kitchen, Peter's first collection will be published by Nine Arches Press in June 2020.

Gregory Leadbetter is a poet and critic. His poetry collections include *The Fetch* (Nine Arches Press, 2016) and the pamphlet *The Body in the Well* (HappenStance Press, 2007). His second full-length collection will be published by Nine Arches Press in 2020. His book *Coleridge and the Daemonic Imagination* (Palgrave Macmillan, 2011) won the University English Book Prize 2012. He is currently Reader in Literature and Creative Writing at Birmingham City University.

Harry Man won the UNESCO Bridges of Struga Award. His pamphlet *Lift* was shortlisted for a Best New Pamphlet Sabotage Award and his second, *Finders Keepers*, illustrated by the artist Sophie Gainsley was shortlisted for the Ted Hughes Award for New Work in Poetry. His latest book is *Thereafter / Deretter* and is co-written with the poet Endre Ruset (Flamme Forlag). You can find more of his work at www.manmadebooks.co.uk

Karen McCarthy Woolf's poems are translated into Spanish, Italian, Swedish and Turkish and she makes collaborative work with artists, musicians and film-makers. Her first collection *An Aviary of Small Birds* is described as an "extraordinarily moving and technically flawless" (*The Poetry Review*) "pitch perfect" début (*Guardian*); her second, *Seasonal Disturbances,* explores nature, migration, the city and the sacred. She is a Complete Works Fellow, Fulbright scholar, broadcaster and critic, and has edited five literary anthologies.

Roy McFarlane is a poet and former community worker. He has held the role of the Birmingham Poet Laureate. His debut collection, *Beginning With Your Last Breath*, was published by Nine Arches Press in September 2016, followed by *The Healing Next Time*, a Ted Hughes Award and Jhalak Prize nominee, and a Poetry Book Society recommendation. He is presently a Jerwood Bursary recipient, looking at the mothers and daughters of Windrush.

Clare Pollard has published five collections of poetry, most recently *Incarnation*. Her play, *The Weather*, premiered at the Royal Court Theatre. Her translations include *Ovid's Heroines*, which she toured as a one-woman show, and a co-translation of Asha Lul Mohamud Yusuf's The Sea-Migrations, which was *The Sunday Times* Poetry Book of the Year in 2017. She edits *Modern Poetry in Translation*. Her latest book is non-fiction, *Fierce Bad Rabbits: The Tales Behind Children's Picture Books* (Fig Tree).

Peter Raynard is editor of Proletarian Poetry: poems of working class lives. He has had two books of poetry published, *Precarious* (Smokestack Books) and *The Combination: a poetic coupling of the Communist Manifesto* (Culture Matters). His next poetry book will be published by Nine Arches Press in 2021.

Roger Robinson has performed worldwide and is an experienced workshop leader and lecturer on poetry. Chosen by Decibel as one of 50 writers who have influenced the black British writing canon. He was shortlisted for the OCM Bocas Poetry Prize, the Oxford Brookes Poetry Prize, and highly commended by the Forward Poetry Prize 2013. He is a co-founder of both Spoke Lab and the international writing collective Malika's Kitchen, and an alumnus of The Complete Works.

Jacqueline Saphra's *All My Mad Mothers* from Nine Arches Press was shortlisted for the 2017 TS Eliot prize. In the same year *A Bargain with the Light: Poems after Lee Miller* was published by Hercules Editions. *Dad, Remember You Are Dead* was published Nine Arches in September 2019. Jacqueline teaches and mentors for The Poetry School and is a founder member of Poets for the Planet. www.jacquelinesaphra.com

Joelle Taylor is an award-winning poet, playwright, author and editor who recently completed an international tour with her latest collection *Songs My Enemy Taught Me*. She is widely anthologised, the author of three full poetry collections and three plays and is currently completing her debut book of short stories *The Night Alphabet*. She has featured on radio and television, and founded the UK's national youth slam championships. Her work is taught as part of the English GCSE syllabus.

Marvin Thompson was born in London to Jamaican parents and now lives in mountainous South Wales. He works as an English teacher and has an MA in Creative Writing. *Road Trip,* his debut poetry collection, will be published in 2020 (Peepal Tree Press). Marvin's poems have appeared in a number of literary journals, including: *The Poetry Review, Long Poem Magazine* and *Poetry Wales*. In 2016, he was selected for the *Primers: Volume Two* poetry mentoring scheme run by Nine Arches Press.

Julia Webb is a founding editor of *Lighthouse* literary journal and a graduate of UEA's poetry MA. She lives in Norwich where she teaches creative writing, mentors poets and works for Gatehouse Press. She has won the Poetry Society's Stanza competition (2011)

and the Battered Moons poetry competition (2018) and her poem 'Sisters' was highly commended in the 2016 Forward Prize. She has two collections published with Nine Arches Press: *Bird Sisters* (2016) and *Threat* (2019).

Antosh Wojcik is a poet, drummer & sound artist. His cross-disciplinary performance piece, 'How To Keep Time: A Drum Solo for Dementia' was produced by Penned in the Margins and toured the UK and internationally, supported by Arts Council England, in 2019. He has also led (B)old Words, a poetry group for those with a dementia diagnosis at the National Poetry Library, South Bank, facilitating writing sessions, editing an anthology and curating a sound installation for the London Literature Festival.

ACKNOWLEDGMENTS

Liz Berry: essay includes material previously published in *Spake: Dialect and Voices from the West Midlands* (Nine Arches Press, 2019).

Debjani Chatterjee's poems 'Enterprising Harmony' (from J*ade Horse Torso,* Sixties Press, 2003.) and 'An 'Indian Summer'' (from *Namaskar: New & Selected Poems,* Redbeck Press, 2004) included by kind permission of the poet.

Peter Kahn: essay includes material from previously published pieces found on LitHub and the Poetry Society's website. A special thanks to Raymond Antrobus and Helen Bowell.

Roy McFarlane: quoted poems from *Olio* by Tyehimba Jess (Wave Books, 2016), included by permission of the publishers, with many thanks. www.wavepoetry.com.

Jacqueline Saphra: Edna St. Vincent Millay, 'I will put Chaos into fourteen lines' from Collected Poems. Copyright 1954 and renewed © 1982 by Norma Millay Ellis. Reprinted with the permission of The Permissions Company, LLC on behalf of Holly Peppe, Literary Executor, The Millay Society. www.millay.org.